ALMOST PIONEERS

One Couple's Homesteading Adventure in the West

LAURA GIBSON SMITH

Edited by John J. Fry

To Phyllis —
Hope that you enjoy
Laura's book.
Best wishes!
John J. Fry

TWODOT®

GUILFORD, CT
HELENA, MONTANA
AN IMPRINT OF GLOBE PEQUOT PRESS

TWODOT®

To buy books in quantity for corporate use
or incentives, call **(800) 962-0973**
or e-mail **premiums@GlobePequot.com.**

TwoDot is an imprint of Globe Pequot Press and a registered trademark of Morris Book Publishing, LLC.

Layout: Casey Shain
Project editor: Lynn Zelem
Map by Melissa Baker, © Morris Book Publishing, LLC

Library of Congress Cataloging-in-Publication Data
Smith, Laura Gibson, 1891-1973.
Almost pioneers : one couple's homesteading adventure in the West /
Laura Gibson Smith ; edited by John J. Fry.
      pages cm
 Includes index.
 ISBN 978-0-7627-8439-4
 1. Smith, Laura Gibson, 1891-1973. 2. Smith, Earle Sloan, 1890-1985.
3. Frontier and pioneer life—Wyoming—Laramie County. 4.
Pioneers—Wyoming—Laramie County—Biography. 5. Laramie County
(Wyo.)—Social life and customs. 6. Laramie County (Wyo.)—Biography.
I. Fry, John J., editor. II. Title.
 F767.L3S65 2013
 978.7'19—dc23
                                                          2012046529

Printed in the United States of America

10 9 8 7 6 5 4 3 2 1

To Paula
Again, and always.

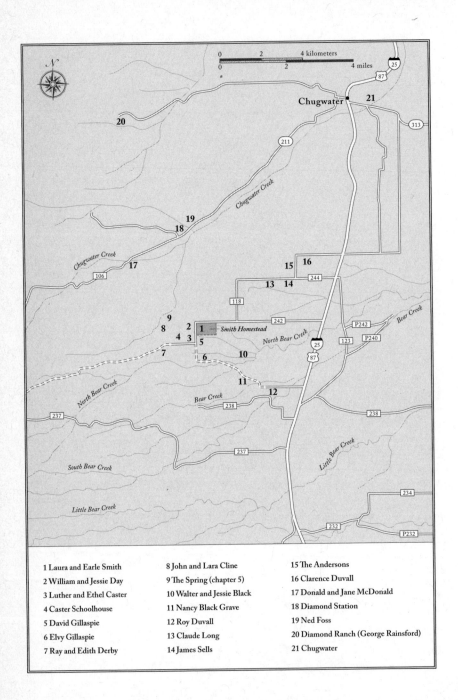

1 Laura and Earle Smith
2 William and Jessie Day
3 Luther and Ethel Caster
4 Caster Schoolhouse
5 David Gillaspie
6 Elvy Gillaspie
7 Ray and Edith Derby
8 John and Lara Cline
9 The Spring (chapter 5)
10 Walter and Jessie Black
11 Nancy Black Grave
12 Roy Duvall
13 Claude Long
14 James Sells
15 The Andersons
16 Clarence Duvall
17 Donald and Jane McDonald
18 Diamond Station
19 Ned Foss
20 Diamond Ranch (George Rainsford)
21 Chugwater

Contents

Preface

by John J. Fry

I teach history to undergraduates. I don't often require them to read the scholarly introductions to the historical books I assign. They are happy that they have fewer pages to read. I want them to encounter the source directly, without being told what to expect or what it all means. They need to learn how to figure it out for themselves.

As a result, I have decided against providing a lengthy introduction to this work by an Iowa woman who homesteaded with her husband in Wyoming. Laura Smith's prose is direct and understandable. She has an excellent ear for description, narrative, and dialogue. The book also displays a good feel for suspense and a well-timed sense of humor. Above all, Laura is an entertaining storyteller. There is not much reason for me to provide extensive background; instead, I will provide as little as possible so that the reader can listen to Laura tell her story.

Laura Gibson and Earle Smith were born in rural central Iowa in the 1890s. They met in high school and were married in Chicago in 1911. From 1913 to 1916, they lived on a 320-acre homestead in southeastern Wyoming. They then moved back to Iowa, where they lived most of the rest of their lives. Sometime later, Laura wrote this memoir and named it *Almost Pioneers*. Laura and Earle's hopes, dreams, and motives are revealed slowly over the course of the book.

I have provided footnotes that explain some of the people, places, and events they encountered, along with some comments about historical context. However, I have placed my broader interpretation of the text and its significance in the afterword. I realize that I run the risk of readers not reading most of what I myself have written, but I hope that after you have read her book, you will be interested in discussing it with someone. At this point, let it suffice to say that I believe this story of one family's experience in the West is in fact the story of many Americans. It reveals truths not only about the several thousand dry farmers that moved to Wyoming in the early twentieth century, but also about the hundreds of thousands of families who moved west during this country's history. Additionally, however, the Smiths are representative of all Americans who are willing to go backward to go forward, willing to launch out into the unknown in order to move closer to realizing their dreams. Laura joined dozens of other American women who wrote about their experiences as a way of remembering them, understanding them, and sharing them with others. I hope that you enjoy reading her book as much as I enjoyed working with it.

I would like to place my thanks at the beginning of the book to show my gratitude to all who have enabled me to bring Laura's manuscript to publication. First and foremost is my wife, Paula, to whom this book is dedicated. She took care of our family when I made research trips to Iowa and Wyoming. She helped me in a myriad of ways as I worked on the manuscript, taught full-time, and served a variety of nonprofit organizations. Her talents are many more than I can describe in a short space, and I thank God for placing her in my life. I also thank my children—Deborah, Stephen, Benjamin, and Daniel—for sharing me with this project. And I thank God the Father for giving me every spiritual and physical blessing in my Lord Jesus Christ, including the incredible opportunity to serve Him by teaching and writing.

Thanks are due to Cathy and Michael Wheatcraft for their assistance on the Iowa end of things. Michael is the son of Laura and Earle's son Bertel Smith's second wife. Cathy and Michael found the manuscript when they bought Bert's house after his death. They donated it and other items from Laura's life to the Iowa Women's

Archives, where I first read it. They also provided me with background information on Laura and Earle. Thanks to Michael and his brother William Wheatcraft for their support of the project. Thanks to Alan Andersen for providing the initial editing of the manuscript during the 1980s, and for his encouragement.

In Wyoming, many thanks to Dean and Ruth Vaughn and Clyde and Frances Caster for hosting me, for taking me to the locations described in the book, and for answering dozens of my questions. And thanks to Phil Roberts of the University of Wyoming, who was a source of many insights about the history of Wyoming, and of encouragement to stay with the project. Thanks to Phil, John Miller, and Alan Andersen for graciously reading the entire manuscript and making many good suggestions. Any errors are my responsibility, not theirs.

Historians can't do what we do without the assistance of librarians and archivists. Many thanks to the staffs of the following, in alphabetical order: the American Heritage Center at the University of Wyoming, the Ames Historical Society, the Cook County Clerk's Office, the Drake University Law School Library, the Iowa State University Library, the Iowa Women's Archives at the University of Iowa, the Laramie County Clerk's Office, the State Historical Society of Iowa in Iowa City, the State Library of Wyoming, the University of Iowa Law School Library, and the Wyoming State Archives. Thanks also to the American Heritage Center, the Chugwater Museum, the Iowa Women's Archives, and the Wyoming State Archives for granting me permission to use their photographs. Finally, thanks to Barbara Mayes Boustead, a climatologist at the National Oceanic and Atmospheric Administration / National Weather Service, for sending me extensive weather data for Chugwater.

Thanks very much to Rita Rosenkranz of the Rita Rosenkranz Literary Agency and Erin Turner at Globe Pequot Press. Without them, this book would not have seen publication. Thanks also to Jennifer

Kroll, Melissa Hayes, and Lynn Zelem at GPP, whose attention to detail improved the book in countless ways.

Thanks to the faculty development committee, provost, president, and board of directors of Trinity Christian College for their support of this project financially through Trinity Research Fellowships, summer grants, and travel support. Thanks to my colleagues in the history department, Bob Rice and David Brodnax Sr. Finally, thanks to my colleagues in other departments who listened to me talk about different parts of the book, asked me questions, and helped me to improve my analysis. Special thanks to Liz Rudenga, Derrick Hassert, Mackenzi Huyser, Dave Klanderman, Craig Mattson, and George Pierson for their support and encouragement. It is a privilege and a pleasure to work alongside everyone at Trinity.

BLUE ISLAND, ILLINOIS
July 2012

Earle and Laura Smith in the mid-1910s. LAURA GIBSON SMITH PAPERS, IOWA WOMEN'S ARCHIVES, UNIVERSITY OF IOWA LIBRARIES

FOREWORD
by Earle Smith[1]

WHEN I WAS A SOPHOMORE AT AMES HIGH SCHOOL, I USED TO STAY out all night with the boys, "bumming around." Percy Ellis and I got into all sorts of mischief with the trains, hopping a freight train to Marshalltown or Boone where we could buy a good hamburger for a nickel. There were no good restaurants in Ames at that time. But then my mother got remarried and I had to settle down.[2]

Laura and I met in 1907 when I was a junior in high school and she was a sophomore. Percy Ellis was going with a girl named Myrtle Hubbard. Laura's family had just moved back to Iowa from California, and Laura and Myrtle had gotten to be good friends.[3]

Laura was a year behind me in school. It happened that I was taking extra courses, and I was in one class with Laura. There were two new girls in the class, Laura Gibson and Eva Cox, who were both from out of town.[4] Laura was wearing a red skirt. I knew that she and Myrtle were friends, so I said to Percy, "I'd like to have a date with the girl in the red skirt."

---

1 Earle Smith wrote this foreword with the help of Alan Anderson in 1983. See the afterword for a complete chronology of the manuscript.

2 Percy Ellis graduated with Earle Smith in June of 1909 ("Ames High Graduates 56," *Ames Times,* May 13, 1909).

3 Myrtle Hubbart (not Hubbard) appears in the 1900 and 1910 census for Ames; she was born in September of 1889, and graduated with Earle in June of 1909 (1900 and 1910 US Census, www .ancestry.com, accessed March 6, 2008; "Ames High Graduates 56").

4 Eva Cox was born in Iowa, but her father was from Illinois and her mother was from Wisconsin. She graduated with Laura in June 1910 (1910 US Census, www.ancestry.com, accessed March 6, 2008, "High School Commencement June 2," *Ames Times,* May 26, 1910; "H.S. Students Form Plans," Ames Times, June 9, 1910).

Laura always kidded me about asking for "the girl in the red skirt." I didn't even remember her name then. Myrtle arranged the date.

There were three couples of us that used to run around together. We would go out and wander along the Skunk River in the northeast part of town—that was all there was to do in those days. Then in the evenings, we'd all go to Laura's house where she'd play the piano and we'd all sing and pull taffy.

When I was a senior and Laura was a junior, we were on the Debating Team together. We once made the front page of the *Ames Times* for winning a debating contest. I was also the president of the "Dissenters," the boys' literary society, and Laura was president of the "Juntos," the girls' society.[5]

When I got out of high school, I worked a year at Bosworth's Drug Store on the south side of Main Street in Ames. I'd worked there my senior year during my time off and during the summer. Percy Ellis had gotten ahead with his schoolwork and had all his credits, so he was able to graduate midseason and work in the drugstore. That summer, the owner of the store wanted to remodel and make an apartment upstairs, so he hired me to help around. Then Percy decided he wanted to go out and sell aluminum, so I took over his job at the drugstore during Laura's senior year. After Laura graduated, she taught country school and I went to Drake University Law School.[6]

I was twenty and she was twenty when we got married. Laura had gone to Wisconsin with her mother to visit her family. She had then gone to Chicago and was staying with her brother. I was a reporter on

---

5   "High School Debaters Who Have Won Two Big Victories" (Ames *Times*, January 28, 1909). For more on Laura and Earle's high school years, see the afterword.

6   Bosworth's Drug Store advertised that they were "Headquarters for Drugs, Books, Medicines, Cigars, Wall Paper, and Paints" (Ames *Times*, July 15, 1909). Earle only attended Drake for one year (*Alumni Directory of the Drake University Law School, 1881–1956* [Des Moines: Drake University, 1956], 20; *Alumni Directory, Drake Law School, 1973* [Des Moines: Drake University, 1973], 52).

the *Ames Times* for summer work. One day Percy Ellis came in and said, "Listen, there's a round-trip train from Story City to Chicago for five dollars, plus one dollar each way for the tourist Pullman." So we decided to go.[7]

I wrote Laura and told her I was coming.

When we got to Chicago, Laura came down to meet us. I said, "Why don't you go out with us, Percy?"

He said, "No, I'll just wander around. You kids go and do what you please."

So Laura and I went down to the Chicago Art Institute. We sat there in front, looking around, wondering what to do. We decided that we'd get married. We'd never thought of getting married before we got to Chicago. So we went over to get the license. I had to lie a little when I got the license; I said I was twenty-one.

We thought we'd keep our marriage a secret until we finished school,[8] but it didn't work. The courthouse reporter in Chicago turned out to be a person we knew. He had graduated from the Journalism Department at Iowa State and had worked on a local paper, so he knew both of us. He wasn't there when we got the license, but right after we left he came in and happened to see our name, so he wired it to the *Des Moines Capital*. They put the story on the front page.

We had a hell of a time finding a preacher; Laura wanted a Methodist preacher. Before we had even found one, the story had made the afternoon edition back home.

---

7   This was most likely the Chicago and Northwestern Railroad, which ran to Ames and then east. It could have been the Iowa Central, which ran to Marshalltown and then connected to the Chicago and Northwestern (*Standard Historical Atlas of Mitchell County Iowa* [Chicago: Anderson Publishing, 1911]).

8   Several secret marriages were reported in the *Ames Times* in previous years (" 'I'm Married Now' Said She," *Ames Times*, November 11, 1909; "Another Nevada Pipe Dream," *Ames Times*, March 16, 1911).

We took the Elevated to the north, got off somewhere, and wandered around until we finally found a Methodist preacher. He was an old man, and there were two old women, his wife and his wife's sister, who were our witnesses.

When we got back, Percy met us at the hotel at suppertime. I wanted to pay for our meals, since it was our wedding dinner. Percy said to me, "Why in hell are you insisting on paying for the whole meal?"

I said, "Oh, this is just something else that Laura wants. I'll pay for this dinner." That was our wedding dinner, and Percy Ellis didn't know it.

When I got back to Ames and got off the train, I noticed everyone was looking at me as I walked down the street. I wondered why. I went straight from the depot to my office at the *Ames Times*. When I walked in, everyone jumped on me and said, "You been married?"

I said, "No."

Percy had gone somewhere when he got off the train. When he walked in, they all said, "Was Earle married in Chicago?"

And he said, "No, why?"

They got out the paper and showed us the front page of the *Des Moines Capital*: EARLE SMITH AND LAURA GIBSON OBTAIN A MARRIAGE LICENSE IN CHICAGO.[9]

This was something that couldn't happen again in a million years—to have somebody in Chicago that knew both of us and was a reporter at City Hall where we got the license. We were married for sixty-two years and three months, so our marriage worked out.

---

9   Unfortunately, I have not been able to document this story. I did obtain a copy of their marriage license from Cook County, Illinois, Vital Records; it certifies that Laura and Earle were married on Monday, July 24, 1911. However, I was not able to find the article mentioned here in extant issues of the *Des Moines Capital*, the *Des Moines Tribune*, or the *Des Moines Register* and *Leader*. The *Capital* did sometimes print afternoon extra editions, and not all of them are preserved on microfilm, so it is possible that the article was in the afternoon edition of that paper for July 24.

I taught at a country school near Zearing while Laura went to Capital City Commercial College in Des Moines, which is now A. I. B.[10] When Laura finished college, we both went to Moravia to teach. It is there that Laura begins our story. . . .

---

10 Capital City Commercial College was founded in 1885. It offered courses in bookkeeping, shorthand, and other subjects. A. I. B. College of Business was founded in 1921, and when Capital City closed due to lack of enrollment in 1961, A. I. B. took over some of their records (Joan Bindel, vice president for advancement, A. I. B. College of Business, phone conversation with author, February 19, 2008).

Headquarters of the Swan Land and Cattle Company at Chugwater, about 1918.

CHAPTER ONE

Wyoming

There is a fascination about the vastness of the Western Plains, the rugged mountains, the uncertainty of the horizon, the crispness and clarity of the air, and the brilliance of the sunshine that captures the imagination of anyone who comes to Wyoming, and draws them back if they leave.

In Wyoming's great spaces, winds blow over prairies and mountains sending Russian thistles and tumbleweeds bounding for miles, piling winter snows in deep drifts or melting it like magic. Barbed-wire and buck fences stretch for miles; the atmosphere is so clear that mountains seem near, and stars shine so brilliantly they look to be within reach.

Early in the nineteenth century, Wyoming was marked on the map as part of the Great American Desert.[1] According to Daniel Webster, it was "not worth a cent," being, as he declared, "a region of savages, wild beasts, shifting sands, whirlwinds of dust, cactus, and prairie dogs."[2]

---

1   "Great American Desert" was first used for the Great Plains by Major Stephen Long on the map he created after a federally funded expedition in 1820. The term's continued use for several decades showed that during the early 1800s, many Americans could not imagine living permanently on the immense grasslands. See D. W. Meinig, *The Shaping of America: A Geographical Perspective on 500 Years of History*, Volume 2: Continental America, 1800–1867 (New Haven: Yale, 1993), 76–77 and Richard White, *"It's Your Misfortune and None of My Own": A New History of the American West* (Norman: University of Oklahoma, 1991), 121–122.

2   This quote is given in I. S. Bartlett, editor, *History of Wyoming* (Chicago: S. J. Clarke, 1918), 356, and repeated in the Federal Writers' Project's guide to the state, *Wyoming: A Guide to Its History, Highways, and People, Compiled by workers of the Writers' Program of the Works Projects Administration in the State of Wyoming* (New York: Oxford, 1941), 68. Phil Roberts of the University of Wyoming, among others, believes that this quote is probably apocryphal (Philip Roberts, e-mail message to author, February 20, 2011).

The first homestead entry in Wyoming was completed in 1870. It was not until the late 1880s and early 1890s that a tide of settlement came into Wyoming under Homestead laws. Many newcomers took up land and began to build wire fences. This enraged the large cattle owners who used the open range, for the fences prevented herds from drifting to natural shelter during storms and blocked the way to water holes.[3]

In 1913, my husband Earle Smith and I decided to file a claim in Wyoming. Both of us had been reared in Iowa, which was an agricultural state in the early 1900s, with very few other industries. At the ripe age of twenty-two, we decided to become "settlers."

My father came from Edinburgh about the time of the War Between the States and settled in Jamesville [*sic*], Wisconsin. After their marriage, my parents moved to Iowa to find cheaper land. My father came from Scotland with a craving for a land of opportunity. He had a few coins when he landed. By the time I arrived, the tenth child, he owned a large farm.[4]

My mother's people had come from England in Revolutionary Days. One grandfather came from Holland. My maternal great-grandfather brought his bride from Rhode Island in 1837 by covered wagon, and bought government land in northern Illinois. He paid $1.25 an acre using scrip for the purchase. His bride had "heired" $300, which she used also to buy land. They lived out their days on a beautiful farm. Their sons and daughters moved on west; three of them took claims in South Dakota, and from there went on to southern California, where they all pioneered in raising citrus.

3   The animosity between ranchers and homesteaders is amply documented. See John W. Davis, *Wyoming Range War: The Infamous Invasion of Johnson County* (Norman: University of Oklahoma, 2010), esp. 35–38, 67–77.

4   Andrew Gibson is listed in the 1900 and 1910 US Censuses as being born in Scotland. He also appears in the 1860 US Census, living near Janesville (not Jamesville), Wisconsin (1860, 1900, and 1910 US Census, www.ancestry.com, accessed March 6, 2008). For more on Laura and Earle's family, see the afterword.

Earle's family was practically the same. Of Scotch, Irish, and English ancestry, his people had pushed on west and farther west until they were firmly established in Iowa. To Earle and me, it seemed wholly natural to want land. Any Iowa land cost far beyond our wildest dreams, but if we could obtain 320 acres in Wyoming by merely living on it for three years and putting on a few improvements, we figured that was within our capabilities.

We were married at the age of twenty. We attempted to continue our studies—Earle was in his second year of law at the University, and I was taking a business course—but we couldn't stretch our money far enough. So the second year after our marriage, we both taught school in a small town in southern Iowa. Earle was superintendent of the school and was called "Professor," much to his embarrassment. I taught seventh and eighth grades.

It didn't take us long to realize that we might be old and decrepit before we could save enough from our small salaries to finish college. Earle received $90.00 a month and I earned $40.00 per month for a nine-month school year.

A few years earlier a group of Iowa farmers, some of them from near our town of Moravia, had taken claims east of Chugwater, Wyoming, in an area known as Chugwater Flats. They had plowed up the land and were prospering with wheat and cattle.[5]

The idea caught fire with the farmers around Moravia. That southern part of Iowa had been excellent grazing land, hilly and wooded, with good lush grass. But too much of it had been cleared and plowed, so it was badly eroded and wouldn't produce much of anything. Consequently a number of the farm families were anxious to sell out and obtain a larger farm with better prospects.

---

5   The Chugwater Flats are east of Chugwater; Laura and Earle ended up homesteading to the southwest of town.

Earle came home from the Saints and Philosophers Club[6] that sat around the stove at the drugstore one evening and told me all he knew about the land available in Wyoming, and about the different families who planned to go out.

"Laura, let's go to Wyoming and take a homestead."

"What?" I was completely dumbfounded.

"We can get 320 acres by living there for three years. We have to make some improvements, but not very many. Maybe we could gain enough on it so I could go back and finish my law course."[7]

"Do you know anybody else who is going?" I asked.

"There are a lot of families going from around here. You know this land is badly run-down around here, and the men think they can do better out west. There's Roy Duvall, and some of his relatives; a family by the name of Caster; and even Dr. Day is interested.

"You know," Earle went on, "it will take years of teaching to save enough money to go back to college. I'm getting ninety dollars a month, and you have forty dollars a month. By the time we live through the summer, there won't be much left." That night, as we talked it over, it seemed more like a lark than anything else. Neither one of us had any clear idea of the what the landscape looked like, but I agreed to go.

We have never claimed to be pioneers, those gallant men and women who crossed the prairies in covered wagons when hostile Indians and other dangers were inherent in such an undertaking. The real pioneers were those who settled the West when there was nothing except the wide-open prairies, hills, and whistling winds. There were no neighbors within miles, no source of supplies without a journey

---

6   This appears to be a figure of speech, rather than an actual club.

7   The Homestead Act, originally passed in 1862, enabled individuals to claim 160 acres from the government if they lived on the land for five years and made improvements (built a house and put forty acres under cultivation). In the early twentieth century, provisions were changed to enable individuals to claim twice that much of semi-arid land and shortened the number of years from five to three. For a further discussion of homestead law, see the afterword.

of many days. There were no trails, roads, or railroads. The pioneers had nothing to fall back on except their own brave hearts and strong hands. They hunted out sheltered spots in the low-lying hills, sweet running water, and a wide range of grass for their horses and cattle.

We were not pioneers. We killed no Indians. We shot no buffalo. But we did have a complete and devastating break from the life we were accustomed to. We were settlers.

To us there was nothing strange, fantastic, and certainly not romantic about our decision. We simply had an opportunity to acquire 320 acres of land; that was sufficient incentive. Everyone who was at all successful owned land. The most derogatory statement that could be said about anyone was, "He doesn't own a foot of land." To us, land meant the fertile black soil of Iowa, where corn grew as high as an elephant's eye; every kind of small grain produced a good harvest, and fruit and vegetables added their share to good living.

One warm, sunny day in March 1913, Earle set out on the great adventure of going to Chugwater, choosing a half-section of land, and filing on it. He dressed as all the young men did then. His black Chesterfield topcoat had silk lapels; he wore a white shirt with stiff detachable collar, a white silk scarf, a blue serge suit, and a derby hat.

It was warm and sunny in Cheyenne. The brilliant blue sky, the warm sun, and the high altitude made it exhilarating. He was thrilled to see cowboys tie their horses to hitching posts along the main street![8] Out grazing just beyond the new capitol building were flocks of sheep belonging to Senator Warren, who was undoubtedly the greatest

---

8   Cheyenne was founded in 1867 when the area was still part of Dakota Territory. It became the territorial capital when Wyoming Territory was organized in 1869, and the state capital when Wyoming became a state in 1890. Its population was about 11,000 in 1910. See "Wyoming Timeline of State History," www.shgresources.com/wy/timeline, accessed May 15, 2012; City of Cheyenne, Wyoming, "History of Cheyenne," www.cheyennecity.org/index.aspx?NID=133, accessed May 15, 2012; and Riley Moffat, *Population History of Western U.S. Cities and Towns, 1850–1990* (Lanham, MD: Scarecrow, 1996), 338.

shepherd since Abraham.[9] Earle was up early the next morning to take the Colorado and Southern train north to Chugwater. A few hours later he got off at the little station in the midst of whistling wind and blowing snow. There he was in his Chesterfield topcoat and derby!

The town consisted of the railroad station, a small general store, and a few houses. A few blocks from the railroad station was the home ranch of the Swan Land and Cattle Company.[10] The station agent told Earle that he could probably find accommodations there. Earle struggled through the drifts and driven snow to the house where Mrs. Fox, the housekeeper, took him in, as she did all the other travelers and stray cowboys. The storm lasted for three days; there was no possible chance to look for land.[11]

The *chinook* is a drying wind that blows from over the Rockies and is often the salvation of Wyoming stockmen. When feed for cattle is covered with hard-packed snow on the range, it is not unusual for the chinook wind to melt snowbanks two and three feet deep as quickly as if a blast furnace had been turned on them. These winds can

---

9   Francis E. Warren had been president of the National Wool Growers Association, but was also involved in Cheyenne business and real estate. He served as a senator from Wyoming from 1890 to 1893, and then again from 1895 to 1929. See T. A. Larson, *Wyoming: A Bicentennial History* (New York: Norton, 1977), 130–141; and "Biography," Inventory of the Francis E. Warren Papers, 1867–1974, Collection 00013, American Heritage Center, University of Wyoming, Laramie, Wyoming, http://rmoa.unm.edu/docviewer.php?docId=wyu-ah00013.xml, accessed March 3, 2011.

10 The Swan Land and Cattle Company was founded by Alexander Swan in 1882 and had Scottish and American shareholders. By 1913, it operated twenty-one ranches, controlled almost half a million acres of land in Wyoming, and owned over 100,000 sheep. See Lawrence M. Woods, *Alex Swan and the Swan Companies* (Norman, OK: Arthur H. Clark, 2006), 178–179, 184–185.

11 There are no three-day snows in existing weather observation records for Chugwater in March and April 1913, but if the conditions were "ground blizzard," or wind blowing snow without any new snow falling, then it wouldn't have been recorded as new precipitation (NOAA / National Weather Service preliminary data; Barbara Mayes Boustead, NOAA, e-mail message to author, September 23, 2010).

change the weather in a few hours from biting cold to mild, spring-like conditions.[12]

For three days the blizzard held sway, making it impossible to do anything or go anywhere. Then a warm chinook wind came, and the sun and wind melted the snow like magic. Earle tramped over to the store where he bought a skull cap, pulled it down over his ears, and then put his derby on top. It was a slight protection against the cold.

Sometime earlier, Earle had written to Clarence Duvall, who had taken a claim six or seven miles from Chugwater, and was familiar with the area. Duvall came to the ranch house the next afternoon with his team and lumber wagon to take Earle out to locate a homestead. He charged a small fee, but there was no other way to find what land was still open for filing.[13]

"Say, you're going to be cold in them clothes, ain't you?" Duvall inquired.

"I didn't expect to get into a blizzard," Earle explained. "I haven't needed anything warmer all winter."

Duvall bought a few supplies at the store: coffee, dry beans, potatoes, flour, and a can of coal oil. A man by the name of Hunt was owner of the store, and naturally, he was looking for future business.

"You can't go wrong in settling out here, Mr. Smith. This country is settling up fast, and all of you can make good money. Clarence is a good man to help you find a place, too."

---

12 A *foehn* or *chinook* wind is caused when high pressure on one side of a mountain and low pressure on the other side force wind down the latter slope; the resulting air is warm and dry. "It is known along the Rocky Mountains front as a 'snow-eater' because it not only melts the snow rapidly but also quickly dries the resulting mud." See Tom L. McKnight and Darrel Hess, *Physical Geography: A Landscape Appreciation,* 8th ed. (Upper Saddle River, NJ: Pearson Prentice Hall, 2005), 128. Chinook winds in the Chugwater area are caused by the Laramie Range to the west (*Climatological Summary,* Agricultural Experiment Station, Chugwater, University of Wyoming, Laramie, Miscellaneous Publication No. 33.4, 1970, 1).

13 Clarence Duvall appears in the 1920 and 1930 US Censuses, still living in rural Laramie County (1920 and 1930 US Censuses, www.ancestry.com, accessed August 10, 2010).

There was a faint trail for a short distance, and then Duvall simply headed off across the prairie. The horses sloshed through patches of soft snow, deeper puddles, and then drier spots. When he came to a gully, Duvall kept right on going. The horses might be climbing up one side of the gully while the wagon was still descending the other. It was a rough ride, and cold. Six or seven miles later, and colder, they reached Duvall's dugout. He had literally dug out a small cellar and put a roof over it. He had a cookstove, a bed, and a couple of boxes for chairs. Duvall unharnessed the horses and put them in the shed. Then the men went down into the dugout. At least it was warm down there, out of the wind.

Duvall built up his fire and got their supper, only to find that the kerosene had spilled. So they had kerosene-flavored biscuits, kerosene-flavored potatoes, and kerosene in the boiled beans.

Earle was feeling woefully let down after the blizzard, the cold ride, and the discomfort of the dugout. But like a good salesman, Duvall told him of the success of the farmers in the Chugwater Flats area, and the possibilities of Wyoming land. By the time they went to bed, Earle was thawed out and his feet were dry, so his enthusiasm was roused again.

Like a good host should, Duvall let Earle sleep next to the wall, where it would be warmer. The big difficulty was that every time he moved during the night, the dirt and sand showered down on him from the uncovered wall.

They were off early the next morning after a breakfast of kerosene-flavored food, again simply heading out over the prairie. Duvall had only a general idea of where he was going. He did know that the McDonald Ranch leased a vast acreage of state land, and that it was fenced. South of this fence, the land had been opened for homesteaders, so he headed southwest across the open prairies.

There was nothing but a vast area of nothingness. No trees, no distinguishing hills—just undulating land stretching to the horizon.

They found the fence, following it west until they reached a gate, and went through into the open land where they drove around for some time. To the south they found a half-section which lay east and west along the fence. It sloped up gradually to a long ridge at the south, which stretched the entire mile of length. Then the land dropped off to the south, again into more indistinguishable hills. That was the half-section that Earle decided to file on. I have often wondered whether that fence extending along the north side gave him something to cling to out of that immensity of space.[14]

It looked good. There were a number of ponds scattered through the lower part. Duvall explained that they were old buffalo wallows.[15] The sun shone cheerfully, but Earle was cold, tired, and bewildered. There was nothing anywhere but patches of snow, puddles of water, and short, brown grass for miles in every direction. One half-section looked exactly like every other one. So he decided to take that piece along the fence. They drove back to the dugout where Earle got his suitcase. Then Duvall took him to Chugwater, where he took the afternoon train for Cheyenne.[16]

The following morning, Earle filed at the land office. The die was cast, and he returned to Moravia to complete his year of teaching.

---

14 A section of land is one square mile, or 640 acres. A half-section is 320 acres, normally a rectangle that is one mile by one-half mile. In this case, the long side ran east and west and the short side ran north and south. For an explanation of the land survey system used in Wyoming, see Robert Harold Brown, *Wyoming: A Geography* (Boulder, CO: Westview, 1980), 5.

15 Natural depressions in the ground enlarged by buffalo rolling in them. One authority has suggested that not all depressions identified as wallows by "old Westerners" were actually used by buffalo. See Frank Gilbert Roe, *The North American Buffalo: A Critical Study of the Species in Its Wild State* (Toronto: University of Toronto Press, 1951), 100–105.

16 Earle filed on the "north half of section 23 in township nineteen north of range sixty-eight west of the sixth principal meridian, Wyoming." The township is in the northwestern portion of Laramie County, three townships (about fourteen miles) east of the Albany county line and about three miles south of the Platte County line. Today it is bordered by County Road 242 on the north and County Road 116 on the west (Homestead Patent 573869, Bureau of Land Management, www.blm.com, accessed May 30, 2008; Map of Laramie County, Wyoming, Cheyenne and Laramie County Cooperative GIS, 2008, available at Laramie County Courthouse, Cheyenne, Wyoming).

"I just about gave up the whole idea when I got off the train in that blizzard," Earle told me later. "If Duvall hadn't come in when he did, I'm sure that I would have left. The chinook wind was amazing, the way it took that snow off. It just disappeared! And the day we drove around was beautiful and warm. But golly, those biscuits with kerosene-flavoring . . . I can still taste them!" Earle chuckled. "We had to eat them all the time I was out there at Duvall's."

Soon other settlers from near Moravia went out to file. By mid-summer, every half-section in that vast area was taken. There were a few bachelors, but no single girls; there were some newlyweds, but most of the settlers were families with children. All of them were farmers. Most of them had some livestock and farm machinery which they had shipped out by railroad.

Chapter Two

Diamond Station

The First Homestead Act was passed in 1862 and signed by Abraham Lincoln. Any adult citizen or any alien who had filed his first papers could claim 160 acres of the public domain. He must live there for a term of five years, and he must erect a dwelling, the minimum specifications of which were stipulated in the contract. He must also "improve" the land—which meant clearing or plowing—according to the nature of the homestead. When these things were accomplished, he would be given title.

It was soon found that 160 acres was not enough land in the semi-arid West. For agriculture, a man would need 320 acres for crops, and 2,000 or more for cattle-raising. From time to time, beginning in 1873, experimental amendments to the Homestead Act were adopted. The first of these was an honest attempt to adjust the law to Western conditions, and permitted the homesteader to apply for an additional 160 acres.

Later came amendments called the "Desert Land Act" (1877), the "Timber and Stone Act" (1878), and other modifications of the original homestead law. Meanwhile, the Morrill Land-Grant College Act gave each state 30,000 acres of Western land for each senator and representative in Congress. Other grants went to subsidize railroad construction. Still in circulation up into the 1880s were land warrants called "soldier's scrips," issued to veterans of the American Revolution and all other wars. These could be purchased for much less than face value and then exchanged for land. Coupled with direct

This is the location of the Diamond railroad station in 2008. The station house is gone. The railroad tracks cross a dirt road that goes up through the draw described in chapter 3. This road did not exist in 1913. AUTHOR'S COLLECTION

sales by the General Land Office, the many outright grants comprised the impressive total of half a billion acres by 1887. Almost 100 million acres were in perfected homestead entries by the turn of the century.[1]

The early ranchers gained control of vast tracts of land but did not fence them at first. Their stock wandered for miles, and had to be gathered in by fall roundups. Later, the ranchers fenced their holdings. That was where our area was involved. By joining their fences, the ranchers enclosed great stretches of land that was really still public domain, but which was effectually closed to settlement.

President McKinley appointed Ethan Allen Hitchcock as his Secretary of the Interior. He began a thorough investigation of the entire department, and found incompetence and downright thievery on all sides. Secretary Hitchcock continued in office when Theodore Roosevelt became president after the assassination of President McKinley. Teddy had lived on ranches in the West, and so had firsthand knowledge of the conditions. He sent out the cavalry with wire cutters and orders to cut the illegal fences between every two posts, thus opening up thousands of acres of land for homesteading. It was in such an area that our claim was located.[2]

We moved to Wyoming in August of 1913. It was time to establish our residence on the homestead. We were allowed six months from the time of filing to move in.

We decided that Earle should go ahead to make arrangements for a place to live while we built our house. A young bachelor named

1 See the afterword for more on the Homestead Act and its amendments. The Timber Culture Act (not the Timber and Stone Act) was actually passed in 1873 and amended in 1878. One authority has slightly fewer acres—a little over 80 million—in perfected homestead entries by 1901. See Benjamin Horace Hibbard, *A History of the Public Land Policies* (New York: Macmillan, 1924), 396–397, 411–417.

2 This was not the first time that the federal government had actively enforced laws against fencing federal land. During the mid-1880s, William A. J. Sparks, commissioner of the Public Land Office, filed suits against ranchers and issued orders that illegal fences be cut. See T. A. Larson, *History of Wyoming,* 2nd edition, revised (Lincoln: University of Nebraska, 1978), 179–182.

Maudy Buckmaster from Moravia, who lived on the next claim to the west of us, had built a small shack. He offered us the use of it until we could get our own house built.[3]

Another young bachelor in Moravia named Jim Dawson had filed on a claim, built a small shack, and bought a horse, but had then gone back to Iowa to teach. He'd left the horse behind and said we might as well use it until he came back again. We felt this gave us a little bit to go on, so Earle went out to Wyoming by train in August. A short time later I wrote Earle that I would arrive on a certain day.

Accordingly, I went by train to Cheyenne. I had to stay overnight to get the train north up to Diamond, where Earle would meet me.[4] It was a thrill to stay in the old Inter-Ocean Hotel in Cheyenne. I had never stayed alone in a hotel before. I was up early the next morning and was soon dressed in my best: a blue serge suit with an ankle-length tight skirt and tight jacket, a peekaboo blouse, a large hat, my best black silk stockings, and black shoes. The hotel served a bountiful breakfast of bacon and eggs, hotcakes, and hot biscuits, with plenty of coffee, all for 35 cents. I did justice to my breakfast in spite of being so excited. Then I finished packing my suitcase and walked over to the railroad station an hour early. It was a lovely cool morning in that altitude; the air was crisp, dry, and sparkling.[5]

The train was made up of cattle cars, coal cars, and one passenger coach. That was plenty, since there were only two other passengers besides me.

---

3 This man was back in Moravia, Iowa, in 1915; the 1915 Iowa Census spells his name "Maddie Buckmaster" (1915 Iowa State Census, www.ancestry.com, accessed March 6, 2008).

4 "In Wyoming many people who considered themselves pioneers rode to their frontier homes, not in covered wagons drawn by oxen, but in railway coaches and Pullman cars" (Larson, *History of Wyoming*, 36).

5 The Inter-Ocean Hotel was one of eleven hotels in Cheyenne in 1913. It stood at the corner of Sixteenth and Capitol Avenues and offered "Rooms with and without Bath," and advertised itself as "The Leading Hotel in Wyoming." It was owned by the Burnham Hotel Company and managed by John Brown (*Wyoming State Business Directory, 1912–1913* [Denver: Gazetteer, 1912], 183, 631).

The Colorado and Southern Railroad winds north between low foothills, through the valley along Chugwater Creek. As we rattled along, stopping at every tiny station, my spirits began to sink. I could see nothing on either side of the train but box elder and cottonwood trees along the creek, and beyond, the bare brown hills. No vast herds of cattle or horses were in sight, and I could not figure out what they would graze on if there were any.

The conductor came for my ticket and stopped to chat. "Hmmm . . . Going to Diamond, little girl? Going to visit one of the ranches, or are you a schoolteacher?" he inquired kindly.

"No," I said quickly. "I'm going to live out here. My husband filed on a homestead last spring, and we have to establish residence now. He came out a week ago. He'll be at the station in Diamond to meet me."

The conductor looked thoughtful. "I've heard that a good many people have taken homesteads out beyond Diamond, towards Chugwater. Well, I'll tell you, missus: This train goes back to Cheyenne at four o'clock this afternoon, so if you don't like Diamond, you don't have to stay."

I couldn't figure what he meant by that, but it worried me. Finally, Diamond was called and I got off the train, fully expecting to see Earle waiting on the platform. No one was there.

Diamond consisted of a small wooden freight station. I stepped inside into the tiny waiting room. There was a bench built along one wall. One corner was partitioned off and marked POST OFFICE. That was all.[6]

A nice-looking woman came from the adjoining room. "I'm Mrs. Pete Lingwall," she said. "My husband is section foreman. We live

---

6 The 1912–13 *Wyoming State Business Directory* has this entry for Diamond: "Station on the Colorado and Southern railroad and post office [*sic*] in Laramie County, 61 miles north of Cheyenne. Stock raising the principal industry. Population 10" (*Wyoming State Business Directory, 1912–1913*, 225).

here. I run the post office for Mr. Rainsford, the postmaster. Did you expect someone to meet you?"[7]

"I'm Laura Smith, and I wrote my husband, Earle, that I would be here today. It is nearly a week since I wrote, and I expected he would be here. I can't imagine what's the matter!"

Without a word, she went over to the post office corner and handed me my letter to Earle. "He hasn't been here since your letter came," she said. "Maybe he will ride over today."

My heart sank clear to my toes. This was about ten o'clock in the morning. What would I do if Earle didn't come? I took off my hat and jacket and sat down on the hard bench along the wall.

"Maybe he'll come today," Mrs. Lingwall repeated. "Or maybe someone else will come in and we can send word to your husband. Do you know where he's staying?"

I shook my head miserably. "I have no idea where he might be. He told me to write to Diamond because it's closer to our homestead than Chugwater."

"Very few people except the ranchers come here for mail," Mrs. Lingwall explained. "But if your husband is expecting a letter from you, I'm sure he will be here today or tomorrow."

There are sections of the state of Wyoming where, it is said, you can look farther and see less than any other place in the world. There was nothing in sight except the little station and one big, unpainted, rambling ranch house in the distance.

"Who lives there?" I asked hopefully.

7　Peter Lingwall was born on April 2, 1886, and his wife Julia was born the next year. Both were born in Nebraska to parents who were from Sweden. They moved to Wyoming sometime between 1900 and 1910 (1900 US Census, 1910 US Census, World War I Draft Registration Cards, 1917–1918, www.ancestry.com, accessed March 6, 2008).

"That is the Foss ranch house. Ned Foss is a bachelor and lives there alone," she replied.[8] So there was no possible chance of me staying there overnight. A little thought strayed into my mind that I might have to go back to Cheyenne.

The morning wore on. I sat on the hard bench for a while. Mrs. Lingwall went back to her work in their living quarters. I looked out of each window in turn. There was nothing in sight except the rocky foothills and the box elders along the creek. Magpies darted about in the trees, harshly calling to each other. I couldn't see a trace of a man driving a wagon or a buggy. One cowboy loped past going to the Foss ranch house. Eleven o'clock came and Mrs. Lingwall came out.

"Would you like to have dinner with us, Mrs. Smith?" she asked cordially.

"Oh, yes, I would. I had such an early breakfast that I'm starved. Is there anything I could do to help you?"

"No, I don't go to any trouble. The mister will be here pretty soon. You just rest," she said kindly.

Rest? I couldn't rest, wondering where I would sleep that night! "I think I'll go down there by the creek under those trees. It looks nice and cool."

"I don't believe I would," Mrs. Lingwall cautioned. "The rattlesnakes are bad now in this heat. There are lots of them this year, I think; more than usual. I wouldn't go down there by the creek."

I opened both my mouth and eyes. She chuckled. "Yes, the rattlers are bad in the hot summer. You have to watch all the time. I don't go

---

8   Nadwin Foss was born in Wyoming on October 22, 1889. He had probably recently begun ranching on his own account; in 1910 the US Census lists him as still living with his parents, Frank and Francis (Fannie) Foss and nine other ranch hands (1900 US Census, 1910 United States Census, Social Security Death Index, www.ancestry.com, accessed March 6, 2008).

outdoors very often. One of the men on the section was bitten last week. He's still very sick in the Cheyenne hospital."

I sat down again on the hard bench.

At noon Mr. Lingwall came in and we had a delicious dinner of pork chops, mashed potatoes, and canned vegetables, topped off with dried-peach pie. Mrs. Lingwall had gone to a good deal of work, and I felt that 35 cents was a very reasonable charge for the meal.[9]

Mr. Lingwall was troubled at my predicament. "I think you will have to sleep on the floor here tonight, or on that bench," he said. "We have only one bedroom. But I think sure your man will come today."

I helped with the dishes and then went back to the windows to watch. Nobody in sight. I had one magazine in my suitcase. I reread all the stories and then perused all the advertisements. The bench grew harder. I took another long look from each of the windows. Two o'clock, two-thirty, three o'clock, three-thirty. I thought my watch must have stopped. It was nearly time for the train to stop on its return trip to Cheyenne. Angrily, I made up my mind that I would go back on it.

Mrs. Lingwall came hurrying to the door. "There's a stranger on a horse coming," she announced. "Maybe it's your man."

---

9 It is likely that 35 cents was a standard price for a meal in Wyoming at the time. Using the Consumer Price Index, in 2011, 35 cents would be about $8.20 (Samuel H. Williamson, "Seven Ways to Compute the Relative Value of a US Dollar Amount, 1774 to Present," MeasuringWorth, www.measuringworth.com/uscompare/, accessed May 15, 2012).

CHAPTER THREE

The Big Pasture

I RUSHED OUTSIDE AND AROUND THE CORNER OF THE STATION. IT WAS Earle, but I hardly recognized him. His face was burned and peeling, his lips cracked and bleeding. He wore a big black felt hat, and his clothes were wrinkled and dirty. He got off the horse stiffly. Each of us had the same reaction: We were angry!

"Why didn't you let me know you would be here today?" he demanded.

"Why didn't you come and get the mail?" I retorted furiously. "My letter has been here two days!"

"Well," Earle said slowly, "I don't know what we're going to do. It's nearly four o'clock. It's much too late to go back to the Andersons' to get the team and wagon. It's nearly ten miles from here. It would be dark before I could get back, and we'd be completely lost without even a sign of a trail. This is the first time I've come to Diamond."

"If we had any room, we'd be glad to keep you overnight," Mr. Lingwall said regretfully. "Could you ride double on that horse?"

Earle was uncertain. "This is Jim Dawson's horse he told me to use. He seems gentle, but not many horses will carry double—especially these Western horses."

We tried desperately to think of some other solution, but there seemed to be no other way. I stuffed my nightgown, toothbrush, and comb into the front of my jacket, left my suitcase and Sunday hat in

Draw above Diamond station. This photograph, taken in 2012, shows a little more what the draw might have looked like in 1913. The dirt road is only slightly visible. AUTHOR'S COLLECTION

Mrs. Lingwall's care, and I was ready for the worst. I had a scarf in my suitcase which I tied around my head.

Earle shortened the stirrups and boosted me into the saddle. My tight skirt was clear above my knees; I couldn't do anything about that. I knew this would be the end of my best black silk stockings!

Then came the big problem. Would the horse accept two riders, or would he buck both of us off? I could see us both flying over the horse's head.

While Mr. Lingwall held the horse, Earle climbed cautiously on behind the saddle. Nothing happened. Whatever the horse thought, he did nothing. I attempted a brave smile as I thanked the Lingwalls and said good-bye, but probably I just showed my teeth.

Earle clucked to the horse, swung him around, and we were on our way. I was afraid to wave to the Lingwalls for fear of startling the horse. I'd paid for my dinner, but never could I pay for the sincerity of their concern and sympathy for us.

Dick, the horse, clumped across the plank bridge over Chugwater Creek and then shortly into a draw, which may have been an old stream bed. Sagebrush, weeds, and rocks of all sizes were on each side of the faint trail in the sand. The horse picked his way carefully among the rocks as the trail wound around gullies and big rocks. I twisted in the saddle for a last look at the little wooden station, which now seemed a haven. It was out of sight, shut off by the closing walls of the hills. There was nothing but the hills on either side of the draw and the sky above.

Just to hear the sound of a voice and hoping for reassurance, I asked Earle, "Have you killed any rattlesnakes yet? Mrs. Lingwall told me they were bad this year."

"No," Earle replied. "I haven't seen any—I haven't even heard one. Everybody says that after you once hear a rattler, you'll never mistake that sound for any other."

Just then we heard a faint rattle. The horse didn't shy. Earle stopped him and we scanned the rough ground on every side. Nothing lay there coiled, or slithered away. We started on again. Soon we heard another rattle! Again Earle stopped the horse. We could see nothing.

"I don't like this," he said anxiously. "I'll be glad when we get out of this rough draw. We can't see ten feet ahead with all this sagebrush."

We didn't say a word. We listened. The horse plodded along as though he was accustomed to carrying double. The draw narrowed as we climbed; the hills shouldered close. The horse scrambled up the last few rods and we were out on the great tableland!

In undulating sameness the brown grass extended to the horizon in every direction. There was nothing but the awesome vastness. Not a tree, not a fence, not a house—only brown grass on the endless miles of low hills blending at last into the sky. Not a sound except the saddle creaking and the horse's feet on the gravel. No birdsong nor shrill of a locust. Silence and infinity.

— Once we were out of the shelter of the draw, the wind struck us full force. "Now, we have to find the fence and the gate," Earle remarked.

"What do you mean by the 'fence and the gate'?" I asked. "You mentioned that before."

"Mr. McDonald leased thousands of acres in here from the state and fenced it as part of his pasture. It's all solid, four barbed wires with very few gates. If we don't find the gate on the east side before dark, we can't get out of the pasture, and we can't get to the Andersons'. There isn't any trail. All we can do is to keep the sun behind us and keep going east."

I felt utterly lost. Gone were my high spirits of the morning. The day had been hours long, and here we were, out in the middle of nowhere. We *had* to find that gate! The sun was getting lower. Dick plodded patiently along.

I was fairly comfortable with the stirrups shortened and I could hang onto the pommel. But Earle could only hang onto the reins and let his feet dangle. After several miles, he groaned. "I've got to walk a while, even if I never get on the horse again. My legs have gone to sleep and weigh a ton!"

He got down carefully, stamped his feet to get some circulation, and then started ahead of the horse. He trudged along, the horse plodding behind him. Both of us were silent, alert for snakes.

It wasn't so bad when Earle decided to ride again. I took one foot out of the left-side stirrup, and he swung up behind the saddle. There was still nothing in sight but the long, low hills in every direction reaching to the horizon. Brown grass and sagebrush, with occasional outcroppings of limestone, covered the ground. The shadows grew longer. The contour of the hills changed with the setting sun. We plodded on at a walk. As we topped each rise, we could see Laramie Peak far to the north, with the sun still shining on it. The Peak was our only guide, except for the setting sun behind us.[1]

A herd of cattle grazed in the distance, but they paid no attention to us. At last we saw the fence just as it was getting dark. We were very near the gate. We looked over the ground carefully for snakes before Earle got down to open the wire gate. I was almost afraid to ride the horse through the gate, for fear he would get in a hurry to reach home and would leave Earle standing there. So I shook the reins very gently. Dick ambled through and stopped as I pulled up on the reins. Earle carefully fastened up the gate and we both sighed with relief to know that we were finally out of the big pasture.

I have never known ten miles to stretch so interminably. I knew that Earle was not sure of finding his way in the dark, which was something he hadn't counted on. It wouldn't have taken very long

---

1   Laramie Peak is 48 miles north of Chugwater and has an elevation of 10,272 feet (*Climatological Summary*, 1).

to cover that distance alone on a horse, because he could have loped much of the time, but we had to let the horse walk. It was getting darker and darker.

I shall never know whether Earle guided the horse or whether Dick recognized the homeward direction and chose his own way.

At that altitude of over six thousand feet, the chill comes as soon as the sun is down. We were cold.[2] It was so clear that we could identify the North Star and keep on our easterly direction. Finally Earle recognized the peculiar shape of Whitcomb Hill against the faint light of the sky. That was the first familiar landmark he had seen. It loomed up to the northwest, so he knew we were nearly at the Anderson homestead. At last we could see their light! Never was a light more welcome to anyone. In a little while we turned in at their yard.

The Andersons came out, completely astonished to see me. I practically fell off the horse, and could hardly walk. Earle took Dick to the corral and limped back to the house. To this day that trip is not funny to me, although I can laugh at nearly anything. Mrs. Anderson took us into the house and quickly fried ham and eggs. Home-baked bread and home-churned butter made a feast! Nothing ever tasted better.[3] told Mr. Anderson about the rattling noises we had heard in the draw. He laughed.

"There's a weed that has dry seed pods on it at this time of year," he said. "The wind makes them rattle. They don't sound anything like a rattlesnake, but we're all scared by them until we hear the real thing!"[4]

---

2   Between 1941 and 1970, average lows in August in Chugwater were around 49 degrees, although it did get down to 30 degrees in 1960 (*Climatological Summary*, 1).

3   Charles and Dora Anderson were born in Iowa and had two children (Clinton was fifteen and Marie was ten) in 1913 (1920 US Census, www.ancestry.com, accessed August 10, 2010).

4   Ranchers in the area call this "rattleweed." One assured me that if you hear it close to your leg, "it will make you jump" (Clyde Caster Jr., conversation with author, Laramie County, Wyoming, June 21, 2012).

"I'm so thankful to be here, Mrs. Anderson!" I said. "I began to think we'd be out on the prairie all night if Earle couldn't find his way."

"I wouldn't want to be out all night either," she replied seriously. "It's so cold, and when the coyotes get to yipping, you would be scared to death."

"We'd better all get to bed," suggested Mr. Anderson. "It's late, and you can do your planning in the morning."[5]

---

5   The Andersons, unlike the Lingwalls, had extra space where Earle and Laura could sleep.

Chapter Four

Making Plans

There are various tales about the naming of Chugwater. An old Indian legend says that long before the white men came west, the valley of the cliffs was the home of Wacash, a powerful Mandan chieftain, and his people. One day during the fall hunt, Wacash was gored and trampled by a buffalo bull. Summoning his only son, Ahwiprie the Dreamer, Wacash commanded him to lead the hunt. The son merely grunted and continued to gaze at the white bluffs and dream. Growing impatient, the old chief prepared to adopt another son.

But Ahwiprie summoned the braves to council and spoke of the wasted effort in ordinary hunting. He told them to ride out the next morning, surround the buffalo on the plains, and drive them over the bluffs. The plan worked. As the buffalo fell into the Indian camp, their bodies struck the stones with a "chugging sound." The Indians called the stream "the water at the place where the buffalo chug." The white settler shortened this name to Chugwater.[1]

---

1 Laura's account of the naming of Chugwater is the same, word for word, as that given in the Guide to Wyoming produced by the Federal Writers' Program in 1941. It seems likely that she copied it. See *Wyoming: A Guide to Its History, Highways, and People, Compiled by workers of the Writers' Program of the Works Projects Administration in the State of Wyoming* (New York: Oxford, 1941), 291. The story also appears in Virginia Cole Trenholm and Maurine Carley, *Wyoming Pageant* (Casper: Bailey School Supply, 1946), 97–98; Clarice Whittenburg, *Wyoming's People* (Denver: Old West, 1958), 162–163; and Mae Urbanek, *Wyoming Place Names* (Missoula: Mountain Press, 1988), 39.

　　The only alternate explanation for the name that I have found was in the *Midwest Review* in 1925, which notes that *chug* may have been an Indian word for "beef." However, the article also gives this story with fewer details ("Chugwater," *Midwest Review*, October 1925, Subject File: Wyoming—Platte County—Chugwater, American Heritage Center, University of Wyoming, Laramie, Wyoming).

⸺

We were both tired and lame the next morning, but we knew we had no time to waste with all the work ahead of us.

"What are your plans?" asked Mr. Anderson.

Earle said, "I'd like to hire a team and wagon today, if you can spare them. I want to get Laura's trunk and stuff from Diamond. Then we should go to Chugwater and get supplies. I'll be glad to pay you to take us over to our place tomorrow. I've arranged with Herschel Sells to help me build a house. He's coming in a few days."[2]

"You can't just camp out on a hill while you build a house!" protested Mrs. Anderson.

"We won't have to do that," said Earle. "Maudy Buckmaster put up a little shack on his place last spring. He told me we could use it until we get our own house ready. I saw Herschel yesterday, and he promised it would be only a few days till he finishes some other work, and then he'll be over."

Mrs. Anderson helped me with a list of groceries I would need. "You don't find much at that little store in Chugwater. We order most of our supplies from Cheyenne. But I think you can get along. Get a ham, sugar, flour, and canned milk. You can get dried fruit like prunes and peaches. I'll let you have a loaf of bread."

It was a good thing she made suggestions. I would probably have sent for fresh meat, oranges, and lettuce without knowing any better. But I did put butter, eggs, and bread on the list.

"You've been here over a year, haven't you, Mrs. Anderson?" I asked. "How do you like it?"

"It's terribly lonely," she said simply. "I always thought I was a pretty good housekeeper. But here the wind blows all the time, so I can't keep

---

2   James Hursher Sells was born in 1890 in Illinois; his father was from North Carolina and his mother was from Iowa. By the 1910s, he was living in Wyoming with his wife Ethel. Their son Claud was born in 1911 and their daughter Edith was born in 1912 (1920 US Census, World War I Draft Registration Cards, 1917–1918, www.ancestry.com, accessed March 3, 2008).

the house dusted. I miss my close neighbors. I miss the flowers and trees we had at home. I couldn't stand it, if it weren't for the children. I keep busy all the time with cooking, cleaning, or sewing. Ever since we built the house, somebody has stayed with us while they were looking for land or getting settled. That's made a lot of extra work."

"But you have your nice house," I objected. "And Mr. Anderson says his livestock is doing well on the grass."

"Yes," she admitted. "My husband and the boy like it. I guess it's a man's country, all right. We brought cattle and horses from our farm back east. They're doing fine on this grass, so there isn't any use to fuss. The men wouldn't think of going back to farming like we did at home."[3]

The little girl Jane piped up. "I like it, too. I've got my own horse! I ride all around, and there isn't any school!"[4]

Her mother smiled. "But there will be a schoolhouse built soon, and then you will have to work hard because you've missed a year." The youngster pouted.

That day was spent in getting supplies from Chugwater and my trunk from Diamond. The Lingwalls were much relieved to know that we had gotten to the Andersons safely the night before.

As we loaded our luggage and groceries into the Andersons' lumber wagon the next morning, Mr. Anderson said, "I gave them some coal oil, Mother. I s'pose there's a lantern or something over at Buckmaster's." He paused to think. "By golly," he continued, "you'll have to take some water! I didn't think to have you get a milk can yesterday, Smith. We can loan you a five-gallon can until you get one."

---

3   Women and men did view the West differently. See Annette Kolodny, *The Land Before Her: Fantasy and Experience of the American Frontiers, 1630–1860* (Chapel Hill: University of North Carolina, 1984), especially chapters 5–7, and John Mack Faragher, *Women and Men on the Overland Trail* (New Haven: Yale, 1979).

4   The Andersons' census record from 1920 indicates that their daughter's name was Marie. Perhaps this was a nickname, or perhaps Laura remembered incorrectly.

"Isn't there a well over there?" I asked in amazement.

"I doubt it," Mr. Anderson said grimly. "I don't think Buckmaster had a well drilled. I suspect there's nothing but dirty water in old buffalo wallows. The cattle drink it, but you can't. Might be a spring around in the rough land somewhere, if you can find it."

"Buckmaster said something about a spring," said Earle. "I figure we can get water there." Earle saddled up the horse, Dick. We were ready.

Mr. and Mrs. Anderson rode in front on the spring seat and I sat on a board laid across the wagon box. We took off across the prairie. I know of nothing more uncomfortable than riding in a lumber wagon. It has no springs. We jolted and bounced as the horses swung off across the prairie.

"How far is it to your place, Smith?" asked Mr. Anderson. "Think you know how to get there?"

"Well, I know we have to get into McDonald's pasture through a gate west and a little south of here," said Earle. "That fence runs due north and south. We cut across to the southwest and hit the east-west fence on the south side of McDonald's pasture. There's another gate at the northwest corner of our land. Then it's about a half-mile south to Buckmaster's shack. It's not over ten miles, I suppose."

There was no road; not even a trail was in sight. We rattled and bounced as the horses jogged along. It seemed to me that Earle was lucky to be on horseback. I weighed about a hundred pounds, but I felt like I weighed two ounces. The expanse of prairie looked more vast and empty the farther we went from the Anderson home.

"You'll have to wear a sunbonnet like the rest of us, Mrs. Smith," advised Mrs. Anderson. "This wind and sun burns terribly."

"My face is chapped already, and my lips are cracked," I replied. "I'll surely have to wear something for protection."

"This is wonderful country for cattle and horses," said Mr. Anderson.

"It looks pretty dry to me," I said. "The grass is awfully thin."

Mr. Anderson was ready to fight for his adopted state. "Mrs. Smith," he said emphatically, "this is the finest grass in the world. You look close and you'll see the grass is cured and all gone to seed. The livestock get hay and grain right there. You just look at my cattle. They're rolling in fat, and they haven't had a mite of corn—or anything—but this grass."

I didn't say anything more, but the bunchy buffalo grass still didn't look as good to me as the lush, green pastures of Iowa farms.[5]

"Ever done any farming, Smith?" Anderson shouted.

Earle reined his horse closer to the wagon. "I used to work on a farm during vacations. I've always lived in Iowa where everything is farming. I've ridden horses for years, and I can even milk a cow," Earle yelled back over the din of the rattling wagon. "Laura was born on an Iowa farm, but she's forgotten all about it."

Anderson laughed. "You get you one good milk cow and some other cows. Come next spring you'll have a herd and make money in no time. Better get another horse, too, for the missus."

"I don't think I want a horse," I broke in. "I never learned to ride when I lived at home on the farm. I always feel like I'm up on top of a house when I get on a horse."

"That's just the way I feel," Mrs. Anderson said comfortingly. "I don't go anywhere unless Mr. Anderson takes the wagon. Someday when he gets all the cattle he wants, maybe we can have a top buggy."

---

5   Other Midwesterners were also surprised by the nutritional quality of the short grasses on the Great Plains. Some emigrants on the overland trail to Oregon and California were forced to leave cattle along the way in Wyoming; the next year's emigrants found that the cattle had survived the winter and were thriving on the grass (*Wyoming Voices*, Cheyenne: Wyoming Public Television, 2004, Part I, "11,000 Years to Statehood," video recording).

"Top buggy!" Mr. Anderson snorted. "Where could you go in a buggy? It's rough on a wagon on this prairie!"[6]

"Someday we'll have roads," she retorted. Mr. Anderson shook the reins. The horses trotted and we joggled and jolted in the wagon.

We found the gate in the north-south fence and headed southwest. My only thoughts were of the overpowering immensity of the plains. We could see the faint outlines of the Laramie foothills on the southern horizon. The horses slowed up for a hill and suddenly Mrs. Anderson asked, "How old are you, Mrs. Smith?"

"I'm twenty-two, and so is Earle. He'll be twenty-three in November. I'll be twenty-three next January," I replied.

She laughed. "I would have said you were about sixteen."

"That's just what the conductor on the train said. Probably because I didn't grow very big I look younger. The conductor seemed to think I wouldn't want to stay here after I saw Diamond. He even told me what time the train went back to Cheyenne. I think I'll get used to it," I said.

"Don't you even talk about leaving, Mrs. Smith!" Anderson scolded. "I s'pose it is kinda scary and lonesome for you women at first, but you'll like it same as my wife does."

Mrs. Anderson shrugged her shoulders. "Wait'll you get your house built. Next spring you can make a garden and have a cow to milk. You won't have time to be lonesome."

"I never milked a cow in my life, and I'm not going to start now!" I retorted. "A garden would be fine, but Earle can do the milking."

Still heading southwest, we came up over a hill and saw the east-west fence and unpainted shack.

---

6   "The American buggy was a single-seated, shallow body mounted on a flexible, sprung gear, sporting four lightweight wheels." It was developed in the mid-1800s to deal with bad American roads; many had a removable canvas top. See Thomas A. Kinney, *The Carriage Trade: Making Horse-Drawn Vehicles in America* (Baltimore: Johns Hopkins, 2004), 19–23. The Smiths eventually purchased a top buggy; see chapters 13 and following.

"That's our claim, right south of the fence," Earle pointed out. "It lies a mile east and west and a half-mile north and south. Maudy Buckmaster has the half-section to the west, and Luther Caster is south of him. Dave Gillaspie filed on the claim south of us."

"Looks like it lies well, with that slope up to the ridge all along the south side," Anderson said approvingly. "Got a long valley in there that will make hay for you."

"No rough land on the whole place," Earle added eagerly.

"McDonald's fence on this side will save you a mile of fencing," Anderson said. "And I'll tell you, it's no small matter in work or money to get it all fenced."

We headed for the gate. All the gates were made of barbed wire like the fences, and it was an unwritten law that anyone who opened a gate closed it again before he went on. I always had a hard time with the gates. The end pole of the gate slipped into a loop of wire at the bottom, then the top of the pole had to be pulled and tugged to put it into the loop at the top of the post.

When we reached the little shack, I felt we had reached another haven, although it was not very prepossessing. It was built of rough, unpainted footboards put on up-and-downs. Three windows, one door, and a stovepipe sticking straight up out of the tarpaper roof completed the ten-foot-by-twelve-foot domicile.

Inside was an iron bedstead, a rusty cookstove, a couple of kitchen chairs, and two boxes piled up for a cupboard. Anderson looked around. "Here's an ax," he announced. "And there's a pile of wood outside. That's good; you won't have to pick up cow chips for a while." I didn't know what cow chips were, but I learned later.[7]

Mrs. Anderson looked in the cupboard. "A few dishes and pans. You'll get along all right for a week or so. It won't take long to build your house."

---

7   For those settling on the treeless plains, dried buffalo droppings were often used for fuel when wood was unavailable.

"Looks awfully dirty to me," Jane chimed in.[8]

"There's a broom," I said. "I'll get it swept out in a hurry. And there's a lantern hanging up there. I'm sure we will manage," I assured them. I didn't see just how we could, but I knew we had to.

The men unloaded the supplies, which we piled in the house. Earle paid Anderson for our lodging and for the use of the team and wagon. They agreed that they must get started home. They had work to do, and it was a long way. We watched as they drove off across the prairie, climbed the long hill, and were soon out of sight. As they disappeared over the hill, I felt as though our last link to civilized life was gone again.

"Let's take a look around before we have lunch," Earle suggested.

"I'll have to get some old shoes out of the trunk," I said. "I'm still wearing my best ones, and I don't want to get them completely ruined. My only silk stockings have a dozen runs in them from riding Dick, but at least I can save my shoes!"

So we went out to gloat over the half-section of land that would be ours in three years. Three long years. We trudged nearly a half-mile east and up on the ridge to where we could see all of it. There was no question; it did lie nicely, sloping gently from the south side to the north. We could see there was good grass over all of it.

"I'm relieved," Earle said. "When Duvall brought me over here last March, I'd looked at so many acres of land that I was completely bewildered at the sameness. It all looked alike, and I really didn't have a clear picture in my mind. I liked this place then, and now I still think it was a good choice. See those little ponds scattered through the lower part? The men told me that nearly any year there will be enough water in them for stock."

"But what about for us?" I asked, worried.

"We'll probably have to drill a well," he replied seriously. "That's what Anderson and Claude Long did."

---

8   Apparently Jane had gone with the Andersons and Smiths, although Laura does not explain where she rode in the wagon.

Back at the little shack we took stock. "I'll have to wash these dishes before we can use them," I said briskly.

"Better go slow on the water," he cautioned. "There's only five gallons in that can."

"But Buckmaster said there was a spring back here in the rough land just a mile or so away," I argued. "We can get water there."

"I don't know yet where that spring is," Earle said. "Besides, it isn't going to be easy to bring water here."

I found a dish towel in my trunk, moistened it with a cup of water, and wiped out the dishes and pans.

"Anyway, I don't figure there's anything here for germs to live on, and this will get rid of the dust," I said in disgust. I considered the situation carefully. We needed water to wash; with only five gallons, I knew there would be no baths. I needed water for coffee, plain water to drink, and some for cooking, but water for washing clothes was an unattainable dream.

That five gallons of water was the most precious possession we had. *Five gallons of water.* That can look terribly small. Water was one of the things I had always taken for granted. Water was something that came out of a faucet in any quantity. Or you went to the backyard and pumped buckets full of the clear, cold liquid, or turned on the windmill and let it fill the big horse tank. Five gallons was only twenty quarts, and I didn't know how or where we would get any more. Precipitation varies greatly in Wyoming. The prairies often get less than ten inches of rain per year.[9]

---

9   Some scholars have described 98 degrees west longitude as the "line of semi-aridity"; average precipitation west of the line is less than twenty inches a year, the normal requirement for growing row crops such as wheat and corn. Less than ten inches a year is arid or desert-like. The Smiths' homestead is at about 104 degrees west. Between 1900 and 2010, the average yearly precipitation recorded in Chugwater was about sixteen inches (Walter Prescott Webb, *The Great Plains* [New York: Grosset & Dunlap, 1931], 17–19, 319–384; John A. Widtsoe, *Dry-Farming* [New York: Macmillan, 1913], 24; Robert Harold Brown, *Wyoming: A Geography* [Boulder, CO: Westview, 1980], 112–118; NOAA / National Weather Service preliminary data; Barbara Mayes Boustead, NOAA, e-mail message to author, September 23, 2010).

Both of us were tired and hungry. Earle chopped some wood, very awkwardly, and we managed to get a fire started in the little rusty stove.

I had forgotten to put potatoes on my grocery list, so we had fried ham sandwiches and coffee for our dinner. I felt guilty using water for coffee, but I limited us to one cup each. We munched on a few dried prunes for our dessert.

Long before dark we filled the lantern with kerosene and I wiped out the chimney with a piece of paper. Earle led Dick down to a buffalo wallow a hundred yards from the house to drink and then hobbled him for the night. I had looked at that pond earlier. It was water, but it was muddy. All around it had been trampled into a wide band of mud. Dick was up to his knees in mud before he could reach the water.

I had some bedding in my trunk, for which we were thankful as the chill of night came on. We went to bed early; there was nothing else to do.

Earle chopped more wood in the morning and I managed to get breakfast, although I hadn't used a wood-burning cookstove in years. They had no eggs or butter at the Chugwater store, so we had oatmeal cooked in a minimum of water, with canned milk and bread toasted in the oven.

We began to realize how much we had always taken for granted as we saw how little we had, and how hard it would be to get anything more.

Another day stretched ahead of us, so Earle decided to ride over to see Herschel Sells and find out definitely when he could help build our house.

Chapter Five

On the Prairie

I HAD TO USE A LITTLE WATER TO WASH THE DISHES, BUT THERE WAS NO rinsing. The little shack was only ten feet by twelve feet, so there wasn't much to clean. The hardest part was moving the bed over far enough so I could sweep under it. Not daring to use any water, I wiped off the three windows with a piece of cloth and swept the piles of sand around each window frame onto the floor. There were no shades or curtains, but since nobody lived within ten miles, I figured it didn't make much difference.

I managed to keep busy until Earle returned from Herschel's. I unpacked old clothes from the trunk and put them into the suitcase where we could get them easily, and put our best clothes into the trunk. There was no other place to put them.

I was a bit peevish when Earle got back. He'd had a good dinner at Herschel's place, with all the water he wanted to drink. He'd even washed his hands and face. But of course, he had no way of bringing any home. Herschel had promised to come on Monday.

"I told Herschel I would ride over early Monday morning," Earle said. "We'll go on to Chugwater with his wagon and bring out a load of cement and lumber."

"I'll give you a list for groceries, too," I said. "Some of the things I forgot. We'll need bread, for one thing."

We spent the afternoon figuring just what would be needed in the way of materials for the house. "We'll just build forms against the dirt walls and pour concrete behind it," Earle said. "I plan to get lumber for the forms and then use it for the roof. We can save quite a bit that way. Herschel will know how much cement to get. Where do you want the house built?"

"It seems to me the best place would be about halfway down on the north side," I said. "At least we could see that fence and not have to look at grass all the time."

We didn't know when any other families would come, or where they would locate their houses. So that was our decision. There was a pond near this location that would furnish water for mixing the cement and for stock later.

"You might put up some nails to hang our clothes on," I remarked.

"That's a good idea," Earle replied. "If I had a hammer, I could put up some nails—if I had the nails. But it's a good thing you mentioned it. Put a hammer and saw on that list. And nails."

"It's a good thing we had that inheritance of a couple of thousand dollars to put in the bank," I said. "We couldn't get very far without it."[1]

"We never could have thought of coming to take this claim if we hadn't had that cash," Earle agreed. "We've got to hire everything done that needs horses. I still don't think it would pay to buy horses and equipment, especially this fall. We wouldn't have any feed for them over the winter. There's nothing we can do until spring anyway. We have to have forty acres plowed; that's part of the requirement on the claim. Next spring we'll hire somebody to do the plowing and then rent the land out on shares. Those people over by Chugwater have had good crops of wheat."

So we planned and dreamed, a couple of small, bewildered fish in an ocean of grass. I could understand how trappers or miners develop

---

1   It would have been unusual, but not unheard of, for homesteaders to have this kind of financial backing.

cabin fever. Both of us had depended on reading in our spare time. Now we had nothing to read.[2] There were no tools to do any work. I couldn't do any cleaning, with the water reaching a lower level every time we took a drink. A bath was unthinkable.

Just knowing we had such little water made me thirstier. If we went outside, there was nothing to see but the low hills stretching to the north, to the south, to the east, and to the west, where we could see foothills. One lone tree was etched faintly on the ridge against the sky, twenty miles west. There was no road, no trail in any direction—only a faint path leading to the pond north of the shack.

That night at dusk, the coyotes howled and yelled. The horrible wailing seemed to come from every direction, as though we were surrounded. Earle tried to assure me that they wouldn't hurt anybody, and that probably only two or three of them were making all that noise. But I was frightened. The next morning, early, I saw five coyotes slinking down a little valley to the south of the house. They were trotting along at a leisurely gait, but when I yelled they shot down out of sight in a second.

Earle had been riding to the creek a few miles south, where there was one small tree and a very small stream. We decided we would have to search for the spring Buckmaster had mentioned; the water was nearly gone. Earle took the only pail and I took the largest kettle, which held only about four quarts, and we set out after breakfast.

That blessed fence of McDonald's! It ran east and west, so we could follow it. We walked a long way west until finally we came to the rough land. A path along the other side of the fence showed where the cattle had worn a trail. We figured that trail must lead to the spring. We crawled through the barbed-wire fence and followed this path. At least the cattle had chosen the easiest way to get up and down the

---

2   It's hard to understand why Earle and Laura brought *nothing* to read for these months. For a consideration of several possibilities, see the afterword.

rough hills. We trudged on. At last the path led down a steep bank and then we saw the green of a few scrub box elders. We stumbled and slid down.

There, in all its glory, was a watering tank with a pipe leading into it! Water actually was coming from the pipe. We washed our hands and faces in the big tank; the water was wonderfully cold. We drank from my kettle and stood watching that blessed water flow from the pipe.

Then we heard a bull bellow in the distance and realized with a shock that we were inside the pasture at the cattle's accustomed watering place—and we were a long ways from the fence. It seemed to take hours to fill the pail and the kettle. I watched fearfully for cattle to come from the direction where we could hear the bull. One of the few things we knew about the West was that the range cattle do not like any person on foot.

At last we had all the water we could drink, and the pail and kettle were full to the brim. We started back up the steep hill. The only way to get out was up this 45 degree grade. I slipped, fell, and spilled all my water. I hurried back and refilled it while Earle watched for cattle. The flow was maddeningly slow. Again I started up the steep bank, more careful of my footing this time.

Try our best, we still splashed and spilled that precious water before we reached the smoother cow path. We could hear the bull getting closer. In our hurry to get to the fence, we spilled still more water. Once on the safe side of the fence, hot and panting, we set the pails down. By the time we plodded another mile and a half home, we each had a half pail of water left. We picked numberless grasshoppers out of the water. There were no covers of any kind in the shack. But it was still water.[3]

---

3   Laura and Earle might not have been in any danger. However, a local rancher suggested that "if they were in the middle of the pasture on foot, getting out of there fast was probably a good idea" (Clyde Caster Jr., conversation with author, Laramie County, Wyoming, June 21, 2012).

Another long afternoon stretched interminably. Nothing to read, nothing to do. Earle saddled up Dick. I was afraid to try riding double again. The horse had been tired the evening we came out from Diamond, but he had done little except crop grass since then. I elected to stay at home. Earle rode south, where he discovered a small creek more than two miles away. There were only a few inches of water running there in August.

By Sunday, Earle had such an attack of fidgets that he decided to ride to Diamond to see if there was any mail. We figured it would take three hours, since he didn't know how to get there. All we knew was the general direction of the station.

I watched as Earle rode over the hill a mile to the north and out of sight. Overwhelmed with the immensity and the loneliness of the grasslands, I lay on the bed and cried. After a good cry anyone ought to bathe her eyes with cold water, but there wasn't enough water left for such a luxury.

It was impossible for me to sit inside the tiny shack any longer with nothing to do. I decided to reconnoiter to the south. A low hill cut off the view of the country in that direction, but I had a faint hope that perhaps I could see a tree—or just anything—if I walked to the top of the rise.

I found a long stick in the wood pile and, swinging it in front of me to guard against rattlers, I trudged up a faint path to the top of the hill a few hundred yards away.

Just like the bear who went over the mountain, I saw the other side of the hill. To the east, the rolling hills undulated to the far horizon. In that sharp, clear air, I could see for miles to the south, where a range of foothills lifted to the sky. No trees. Nothing but grass and the wind, blowing a gale.

Then I heard a sound—something between a snort and a whistle. Startled, I swung around. There, within a half-mile to the southwest, was a herd of wild horses. A great, gray stallion was looking straight at me, his head high, ears up alertly, his mane and tail flaring in the wind.

The whistling snort sounded again. For a moment I stood, stunned with terror. Then I whirled, picked up my long skirts, and fled down the hill as though all the Hags of Hades were at my heels. I could already hear the rumble of hoofs. I sped across the swale and sprinted desperately up the slope to the shack. I could hear the thudding hooves coming closer. I thrust the door open, scrambled inside, and slammed the door.

I stumbled to the south window. The stallion was only rods behind me.[4] He came with a long-reaching, easy gait, the mares trotting along behind him with their gangling colts galloping awkwardly beside them. Just before he reached the cabin, the stallion veered off to the east, the mares flowing along in a seemingly endless stream. I rushed to the east window. Without a break in that beautiful rhythm, the big gray led the herd off down through the swale and out of sight behind the hills. I sat down, weak and shaking with fright.

I could see why they used to hang horse thieves without bothering to have a formal trial. A man on the prairies without a horse under him didn't have a chance.

The hours passed and Earle did not come. A dozen times I went out where I could catch the first glimpse of him coming over the hill to the north. Another hour, and another. I was terribly worried. I thought he could easily have gotten lost in that strange country. There was nothing I could do but wait. The afternoon dragged on. Finally, when it was getting dusk, there appeared a lone rider over the hill. I was so relieved that I was angry. It's strange how often relief shifts to anger.

"Did you get lost?" I demanded.

"No, I didn't get lost. In fact, I didn't have much trouble finding

---

4   One rod is about sixteen and a half feet (Distance and Length Converter, www.unitconversion .org/unit_converter/length.html, accessed May 15, 2012).

Diamond from here. Here's your *Saturday Evening Post*. Thank goodness! Now we'll have something to read."[5]

"But what took you so long?" I asked.

"I decided to go on down to the McDonald ranch. It isn't very far from the station, and they insisted that I stay for dinner. The father, Hugh, is a fine old chap. There are three boys and one girl at home. The mother is dead."[6]

"Were they pleasant to you?" I inquired anxiously. "Ranchers are supposed to hate homesteaders."

"They were just as nice as if I owned ten thousand cattle," he said emphatically. "They've been out here for years; they own acres and acres of land. I don't suppose they know how many head of cattle and horses they have. They gave me a lot of information, and offered to do anything they could to help us."

"Here I've been worrying about the ranchers all around here," I said. "I'm really delighted. How old is the girl?"

"I imagine she's about our age. The boys are older. They are real pioneers. They came when there was absolutely nothing here, and made a go of it. They invited us both to come and see them," Earle said happily.[7]

"Now the first thing you buy in Chugwater must be another milk can," I scolded. "Then you can bring a can of water from Herschel's or

---

5   *The Saturday Evening Post* was a hugely successful news and literary magazine. During the 1910s, its weekly circulation was over two million, giving it the highest circulation of any magazine in the world. See Frank Luther Mott, *A History of American Magazines*, Vol. IV. (Cambridge, MA: Harvard, 1957), 671–716 and Jan Cohn, *Creating America: George Horace Lorimer and The Saturday Evening Post* (University of Pittsburgh, 1989).

6   The US Census in 1910 actually listed Hugh as one of the four children of the McDonald family (Robert, Hugh, Maggee, and Duncan). The father's name is given as Donald. It is likely that Laura remembered incorrectly when she wrote this exchange (1910 US Census, www .ancestry.com, accessed May 3, 2008).

7   According to the US Census, in 1910 Robert was twenty-five, Hugh was twenty-three, Maggee was twenty-two, and Duncan was twenty. Maggee would have been twenty-five in 1913, slightly older than Earle and Laura, who were both twenty-three.

someplace, and we'll get this can back to Andersons'. I can't get along this way."

———

Monday morning Earle was off bright and early. That day was not so bad. I knew we were finally getting something done toward our house. Late in the afternoon, Herschel and Earle came home. They had brought lumber and cement—even the hammer, saw, nails, and a can of water in Herschel's horse-drawn wagon.

That was the first time I had seen Herschel Sells. He was a big, handsome man with tremendous strength. I knew we would have our house in a short time.

"Didn't you get bread?" I asked.

"They don't have bread in Chugwater. Can't you make biscuits?"

"I forgot baking powder," I wailed. "But we do have flour." So I made crackers.

Laura, Earle, and the first claim shanty. Their first house on their own land was half-underground. LAURA GIBSON SMITH PAPERS, IOWA WOMEN'S ARCHIVES, UNIVERSITY OF IOWA LIBRARIES

CHAPTER SIX

Cheyenne

THEY UNLOADED THE LUMBER AT THE SPOT WE HAD DECIDED ON FOR our house, brought the cement home, and piled it inside the shack in case it should rain, although that wasn't likely at that time of year. Very early the next day, Earle walked down to the chosen spot. Herschel was there with a slip shovel and spades to square out the corners. The two men dug the twelve-foot-by-sixteen-foot hole for the house and put up the forms. The lower part of the forms were set so closely against the dirt that the cement wall was hardly more than plastering on the dirt.

The second day, working from dawn until dusk, they hauled sand from the draw a half-mile away. Using water from a buffalo wallow, they mixed the concrete and poured the walls. Earle was not used to working with a strong man like Herschel. He tried so hard to keep up that he could scarcely eat his supper and fall into bed at night. Earle had a chance to rest while the walls set, and then they were at it again. They took down the forms and used the lumber to build a peaked roof, then put on rolled roofing and poured a cement floor.

We had three windows a few inches above the ground, windows like old-fashioned basement windows, one each on the east, south, and west. On the north was an old-style, sloping cellar door. A door made of ordinary lumber led into our new house. They nailed boards on the crosspieces over half of the room we intended to use for storage (but which turned out to be our spare bedroom). In one corner of this ceiling they cut a hole. A plank with crosspieces served for a stairway to the upstairs.

The water problem had been solved for a few days with Herschel bringing us a five-gallon can each day, but that had to be used very sparingly. After all, five gallons don't go far.

As we joggled along in the lumber wagon toward our house, I remarked to Herschel, "I wish you would please tell Mr. and Mrs. Long that we would like to have them come over and see us now that we have a house. I didn't want anybody to come when we were in that shack of Buckmaster's."

Herschel roared with laughter. Earle turned a brick-red and looked sheepish.

"What's so funny?" I asked, a bit miffed.

"Haven't you told her yet, Smith?" Herschel asked.

"No, I haven't," Earle replied. "I'm ashamed of myself."

"You'd better tell her the story now while I can hear it," Herschel urged.

"Well," Earle said, "you know Claude Long was one of the few people I knew in Moravia who moved out here. So when I came out to get things ready for you, I got Jim Dawson's horse, as he had told me to do, and then I went to visit the Longs. They had built a barn and were living in part of it while they built their house. They fixed me a bunk up in the haymow where I slept.

"Jim Dawson had also told me back in Iowa to go to his place about ten miles south of here and use his shack and anything there we wanted. So I rode down to his shack. I can see why he would get homesick and go back to teaching in Iowa. He'd built a cabin seven by nine feet; there was a window and a door, but there wasn't a thing left in it. I saw a sheepherder nearby and went over to talk to him. He told me that a tall, thin man and a homely, old woman had come in a lumber wagon and taken everything out of the shack and hauled it away.

"I thought that was terrible, so I went back to Longs', and in all innocence I told them exactly what the sheepherder had said about the tall, thin man and the homely, old woman. They were furious. They said that Dawson owed them a board bill and they'd heard he wasn't coming back, so they went down and got the stuff to cover what he owed them. They thought that I knew they were the ones who took the stuff, and finally told me plainly that anyone who talked like that to them wasn't welcome, and I'd have to leave. Of course I had no idea they were the ones who'd taken Jim's stuff, and I apologized. But they wouldn't believe me."

"Mrs. Long still believes you thought they were stealing that stuff," said Herschel. "I've tried and tried to tell her that you had no idea it was them, but she's still mad at you." Herschel roared again.

"I felt like an idiot," Earle continued. "I had no idea that they were mixed up in it. I thought they had a right to what little stuff there was when they knew he wasn't coming back. He owed them for his board. But I couldn't convince the Longs that I wasn't accusing them of stealing, so I paid them for my board and went over to Andersons'."

"Now you see, Mrs. Smith," Herschel said, "why Mrs. Long won't be over to see you for a while. But she'll get over it. My wife is their oldest daughter. I'll get her to talk to her mother."

"That's a shame," I said, "to hurt their feelings like that. There are so few of us, we've all got to be friends. I hope they will forgive you sometime, Earle."

"They are mighty fine people," Earle said, "and I'm mighty sorry about it."

The Inter-Ocean Hotel, early 1910s. Note the electric streetlights and the electric lights on the corner of the building spelling the name of the hotel.
WYOMING STATE ARCHIVES, DEPARTMENT OF STATE PARKS AND NATURAL RESOURCES

As soon as the house was finished, we arranged with Herschel to take us to the train in Diamond so we could shop in Cheyenne.

"Didn't you ship anything out here?" Herschel asked.

"All we have is a little farm, so we stored everything in Moravia. It will be shipped out with someone who has room in their freight car. We know quite a few folks who are coming out next spring. But for now, we'll just have to buy enough to get along," I replied.

When we got on the train, the conductor grinned at me. "I see you decided to leave. Where's your trunk?"

"We're not leaving!" I said emphatically. "We've built a little house and we're going to Cheyenne to buy a few things to keep us going till spring."

He shook his head. "We'll see if you stick it out three years."

"We plan to!" I said firmly.

Cheyenne looked wonderful to us. It was a cow town at that time, with cowboys and soldiers and horses. It had buildings and street-lights—even electric lights in the stores! It was dazzling after our kerosene lantern. The streets were all gravel; there wasn't a paved street in town. There were hitching posts all over the town.

We stayed at the Inter-Ocean Hotel, which seemed like a palace to us. I took two baths that night, one before dinner and another before I went to bed—and another in the morning. Earle soaked luxuriantly in a tub brimful of hot water. What luxury![1]

The theater in Cheyenne was right up-to-date. It was the old-fashioned type of theater, with boxes. There was a light opera called *Dance Mad* playing that night, and we hastened to get tickets. After a dinner served on dishes evidently washed in plenty of hot water, we went to the show. We had good seats. We were probably the only couple in the whole theater who were dressed casually. The governor and two United States senators were there. Everyone in the theater except ourselves was in formal evening dress! Nevertheless, we lost ourselves in the music and dancing; we could hardly wait to see the final curtain.

---

1   Hotels were vital to nineteenth- and early-twentieth-century community life because they gave the transient American population a place to stay and provided space for public and private meetings. They also performed community-building functions, helping to determine whether a town would become a viable city, especially in the West. See Daniel J. Boorstin, *The Americans: The National Experience* (New York: Random House, 1965), 134–147.

   There is one reference in a local newspaper to Earle Smith staying at the Inter-Ocean, but it was apparently not this visit. The hotel was destroyed by fire in December 1916 ("Earle Smith, Diamond, is sleeping at the Inter-Ocean," *Wyoming Tribune*, May 25, 1914; "Burned Inter-Ocean Hotel Genuine Land Mark Wooly West," *Wyoming Tribune*, December 19, 1916).

One number we shall always remember was the waltz up and down the grand stairs on the stage.[2]

We spent the next day figuring out our purchases. The first thing I bought was a cookstove. We didn't really *need* their best stove, but it was beautiful! I'd never seen anything like it. I was determined to have a pretty range with a warming oven and reservoir. It would have been much more practical to have gotten a cheaper kitchen stove, but I bought the range. It was gray except for the stove top, and had shiny metal trim.

We bought a few dishes, pots and pans, cheap table service, and a teakettle. There were two kitchen chairs, water buckets, a coal scuttle, a lantern, and one plain glass lamp. A sanitary cot with sides that let down was our answer to a couch in the daytime and a bed at night. It was rather unpredictable—it tipped.[3] A bedspring and a mattress finished our purchases. The storekeeper promised to have everything on the train in the morning so we could haul it out home when Herschel came after us.

We made a trip to a grocery store, where we bought a big ham, a slab of bacon, bread, baking powder, dry yeast, and dried fruit. Cans of vegetables finished our list, along with flour, sugar, and canned milk.[4] All of this was to be put on the morning train, too.

---

2   *Dance Mad* was performed at the Capitol Avenue Theatre on November 20, 1913. This seems somewhat late in the year for where this account appears in the narrative. It may be that this trip actually occurred after some of the events of chapters 7 through 9 ("*Dance Mad* Will Be Seen Here Tonight," *Wyoming Tribune*, November 20, 1913).

3   The "sanitary cot" was advertised in many newspapers between the 1900s and the 1920s. It was a metal framed cot with a canvas side or sides that could be folded down and supported. Therefore, it was like a day bed; it could be used as a sofa during the day and a larger bed at night. It is unclear why they were called "sanitary." One historian suggests that the Victorians thought that wood was unsanitary and therefore viewed metal as sanitary. Gillis Harp, e-mail message to author, August 31, 2012.

4   Tin-can technology had been around since the early 1800s, but it was initially expensive and unreliable. The Civil War provided a spur to innovation, and the canning industry took off in the late nineteenth century. See Susan Williams, *Food in the United States, 1820s–1890* (Westport, CT: Greenwood, 2006), 15–16.

Both of us had been completely aghast at the prices charged in Chugwater. We had been living in a small town in Iowa where a five-cent soup bone would make several good meals, where the butcher gave us liver because he couldn't sell it, and where a quarter's worth of steak would serve four amply.

Another luxury we allowed ourselves, even though we hadn't a trace of refrigeration, was two pounds of butter and four dozen eggs. We elected to carry those items with us; they were too precious to go by freight. We returned to the hotel, and I suddenly realized that I would have to have a tub and a washboard. It might be the simple life, but to me it was horribly complicated. So back to the hardware store we went to buy the washboard and two tubs. The salesman tried to show me the superiority of a glass washboard, but I remembered that, long years before, my mother had a corrugated zinc board, and that was what I decided on.

Somehow that washboard seemed almost degrading to me. For years my mother had had a washing machine. When we were teaching in Moravia, I'd hired our washing and ironing done for one dollar a week. Now I would have to rub and scrub on a board.

Had *Dance Mad* been playing that night, I think we would have seen it again. But the road company had left town, so we had to be content.

We had deposited our money in the Wyoming Trust and Savings Bank, which was a subsidiary of the Stock Growers National Bank, so we felt—if not rich—at least secure for a time. Mr. Henderson, the cashier at the bank, made us feel as though we were doing him a tremendous favor by choosing to do our business there.[5] He told us that

---

5   The Stock Growers National Bank was located at the corner of Capitol Avenue and Seventeenth Street. It advertised that "All depositors of this modern bank, whether large or small, receive the same courteous treatment, prompt service, and efficient management of their banking business" (*Cheyenne Trade Review* [Denver: Great Western, 1910], 21; *Cheyenne Leader*, September 18, 1913).

Mr. George D. Rainsford was going out on the train the next morning, and he wanted us to meet him. When we went to the train station the next morning about 6:30, we found Mr. Henderson chatting with a tall gentleman. He called us over and introduced us to Mr. Rainsford.

We were quite overwhelmed that the cashier of the bank should have taken the trouble to come down to the railroad station so early in the morning just to be sure that we met Mr. Rainsford. He was a tall, fine-looking gentleman with a distinctive Vandyke beard. His only concession to ranch life was a large Stetson hat and short boots. His suit, with a cutaway coat, was perfectly tailored. Rainsford had a large ranch where he raised beautiful horses for the Eastern market of polo ponies and coach horses. On the train, Mr. Rainsford paused at our seat and invited us cordially to visit his ranch sometime. He then went on to sit with some acquaintances. In the years after, we were always treated like privileged characters by Mr. Rainsford.[6]

When we got back to the station at Diamond, I had a pleasant visit with Mrs. Lingwall while we waited for Herschel to arrive with his team and lumber wagon. Earle was outside watching to see that our purchases were unloaded safely.

I told Mrs. Lingwall about my trouble with the water and cooking.

"How did you like your ride with two on one horse?" Mrs. Lingwall chuckled.

"It wasn't so bad for me, except that I was so scared. But Earle got tired with his legs hanging down and no stirrups. So he walked a good share of the way and led the horse."

"Oh, my," she exclaimed. "Wasn't he afraid of snakes?"

"Yes, we thought we heard them all the time. Mr. Anderson told us about those dry pods that make you think you hear a rattler. But we haven't seen a snake yet."

6   George Rainsford was an architect and civil engineer who moved to Wyoming to raise horses there in the 1870s. Laura describes a visit to his ranch in chapter 15 ("George D. Rainsford," *Chugwater News*, February 13, 1936).

I showed her my straw hat. "Mrs. Anderson told me I'd have to wear a sunbonnet, but I bought a straw hat that I could tie on. When I was a youngster, my mother tried to make me wear a sunbonnet, but it was always dangling down my back. It was so hot I hated it, so I bought this hat. I'm going to sew some strings on it."

"That's good," she agreed. "I don't like sunbonnets either, but this wind burns terrible."

It was actually fun to get settled in our own little basement house. Earle made a cupboard out of a couple of boxes, and a drop-leaf table from some leftover boards. The lovely new range was set up, the stovepipe was wired to the roof, and we felt quite at home.

But there was still the problem of water. Earle built a sled with a couple of fence posts and some scraps, and used it to haul water from the spring. The wind blew constantly and continuously, hurling sand against the windows, which gradually pitted the glass. There was always a little heap of sand on the windowsills. Earle set a pail outside the doorway one night. The next morning it was gone. He finally caught up with it a mile away.

The Caster Children in 1914. In back: Cecil, Osa, and Wayne. In front: Clyde.

Chapter Seven

The Caster Family

EARLE BUILT OUR SMALL PRIVY ON THE SOUTH SIDE OF THE HOUSE, where it caught the full force of the west wind. But that seemed like the best place, since it was at the back of the house. One morning I went out the door and heard Earle yelling. I looked all around for him, and finally saw that the outhouse had blown over with the door down. The thing was so light that I could roll it over and let him out. Immediately, Earle found some big stakes and wired them outside to prevent this from happening again.

We scarcely had one room settled when, one morning days later, we heard a wagon pull up out front. A covered wagon pulled up to a stop. It was Luther and Ethel Caster, with their baby on the seat. Out of the back came three more youngsters. Close behind was another loaded wagon with two little fellows, Cecil and Wayne, driving it with two cows tied on behind.[1]

Mrs. Caster climbed down wearily. "My, I'm glad to get here," she said. "That's a long ride in a wagon from Pine Bluffs!"[2]

---

1   Luther Caster was born in Kansas in 1877, but by 1885 his family was living in Iowa. In 1910, he and his wife Mary Ethel were in Taylor Township, Appanoose County, Iowa, which includes Moravia, where the Smiths lived in early 1913. In 1913, the Caster children were Osa, age eleven; Cecil, ten; Wayne, nine; Clyde, eight; Wrex, five; and Luther, three (1885 Iowa State Census, 1910 US Census, www.ancestry.com, accessed March 3, 2008; Clyde Caster Jr., conversations with author, Laramie County, Wyoming, May 23, 2008, June 21, 2012).

2   Pine Bluffs, Wyoming, is just over the state line from Nebraska, about forty miles directly east of Cheyenne. "Nearly a hundred miles" is a very good estimate for how far Pine Bluffs was from the Smiths' homestead.

"Nearly a hundred miles," Luther explained.

"We're awfully glad to see you," I said. "It's been terribly lonesome! Come right in. You're going to stay right here while you get your house built!"

"We'll manage," Mrs. Caster said, smiling. "I'm tired of camping."

"We'll have dinner pretty quick," I said. I sliced ham and cooked potatoes. Mrs. Caster had brought bread and butter. After running and racing off their pent-up energy, the children came inside to stand shyly by and watch while we got the meal. We had two chairs and two boxes for the grown-ups to sit on. The older children sat in a row on the couch. I had only four plates, but pie pans and saucers worked just as good. Ethel was anxious to see their land, so after dinner they unloaded the wagon on the ground, took off the hooped top, and covered their goods securely. All of us then piled into the wagon for the ride over the hill to where their half-section cornered on ours.[3]

They quickly decided to build their house a few hundred yards from the corner. "Might just as well be as close to you folks as we can," Ethel said. We were sorry that we hadn't built our house nearer the corner joining their land, so we could have been in sight of each other.

The Casters stayed with us for two weeks. Each night we moved out all the furniture except the cupboard and stove. Luther, Ethel, and the baby slept on the sanitary cot. A mattress on the floor took care of the other five children, sleeping crosswise. Earle and I climbed the chicken ladder in the corner and slept upstairs in the loft. The springs and mattresses on the floor made a very comfortable bed, although there was less than enough room to get undressed. Each morning, the men carried out the mattress and we closed up the cot. They brought the table and chairs back in, and we were set for the day.

---

3   The Casters homesteaded the south half of section 22 of the township (Clyde Caster Jr., conversations with author, Laramie County, Wyoming, May 23, 2008, June 21, 2012).

Ten people in one small room, eleven feet by fifteen feet;[4] but we managed beautifully. The first evening Ethel said, "I wonder if we ought to bake bread tomorrow. The children eat so much bread. Let's save the potato water."

"I've got plenty of flour," I said. "And some yeast. I had to make biscuits because I've never baked bread."

"I brought some starter, and I've got flour, too," said Ethel. "We'll have to get it started tonight." So began my first lesson in bread baking.

I hadn't thought about the small size of the oven in my beautiful new range, but Ethel decided she could only bake four loaves of bread at a time. She baked four loaves of bread the next day, and every day while they were with us she turned out the same number of loaves. The bread disappeared every day as fast as she baked it. She baked lovely bread each day, and saved some of the sponge for the next baking day.

I was still wrestling with getting the right amount of fuel and setting the dampers in the stove properly. But Ethel seemed to know instinctively just how to get the oven heated to bake those delicious big loaves of bread just right.

That first afternoon we didn't get much done but haul water in barrels from the spring and help the Casters make their plans. The family was all tired. Luther said that their horses would have to rest that day.

"I'll have to wash some things for the baby in the morning," Ethel said. "Where will I hang them?"

"We put that barbed-wire fence around the house to keep the wild horses out," I said. "That's where I hang my clothes."

At daybreak the next morning, the two men and two older boys left for Chugwater to get materials for their house. "The horses are still tired from that long trip from Pine Bluffs," Luther worried. "But we've got to hurry with the house. There's so much else to do before winter."

---

4   At the beginning of chapter 6, Laura describes Earle digging "a twelve-foot-by-sixteen-foot hole for the house." The dimensions given here probably mean that the walls of the house were about six inches thick.

The Caster extended family in 1922. Osa had married a local homesteader, Albert Engelker, and they had a daughter named Pauline. Ethel's mother Lydia Beatty was also homesteading nearby. Back row, left to right: Pauline Engelker, Albert Engelker, Osa Engelker, Wayne Caster, Cecil Caster, Clyde Caster, Wrex Caster, James Caster. Front Row, left to right: Lydia Beatty, Luther Caster, Ethel Caster. CHUGWATER MUSEUM

Almost twenty miles to Chugwater across the rough prairie was a long haul, but they brought back all the materials they could. It took several days to bring the lumber, cement, roofing, and other things that were necessary to start building their house.

Ethel and I kept busy with cooking and taking care of the children. The oldest girl, Osa, was eleven—and she was worth twice as much as I was when it came to cooking or minding the baby.

The second day Ethel said, "Now you're not going to use up all your ham while we're here. It'll last a long time for the two of you. I've got a whole sack full of beans. We'll have boiled beans today. Osa, you put some beans on to cook while the bread is baking. We don't need any meat."

From then on our regular fare was oatmeal and bread for breakfast and boiled beans, potatoes, and bread and butter for dinner. Ethel made gravy by browning some lard in a frying pan. She thickened it with flour and added water. It was good either on bread or potatoes. We were all young and working hard. Everything tasted good.

Luther was a short, wiry man, and Ethel was a small, thin, hardworking woman. They had five boys and one girl.

They built their house much like ours, but didn't make the basement as deep and had larger windows. They built the house sixteen feet by twenty-four feet, and put on a flat roof covered with rolled roofing so they could add another story the following spring.

Luther and Earle soon grew tired of hauling water to mix cement. As soon as he could find a well driller, Luther had a well put in. They had to drill about 125 feet before they got water. We were all thrilled about the well, but it was far too deep to pump by hand, so Luther had to get a windmill. There seemed to be no end to what must be done before winter: fencing to keep the stock in, a shed for the horses and cows. The family's two older boys, Cecil and Wayne, were only ten and nine years old, but together they did a man's work. Finally, the Casters were all moved into their new home.

CHAPTER EIGHT

The First Fall

TIME DRAGGED THAT FIRST FALL ON THE CLAIM. AND YET THE DAYS passed rapidly, too. Earle worked every day helping Luther, but I had little to do. We had constant moaning wind that carried off anything that was not fastened down. Sand battered and pitted the window glass, leaving windrows of fine sand on the sills.

The sun was brilliant and warm. The nights soon grew cold at that altitude of five thousand feet. All the small birds were gone. We saw a few flocks of geese and ducks going south in search of winter quarters.

I had two big problems: keeping a fire going in the cookstove and learning devious ways of conserving water. When I baked bread, I either wouldn't have the oven hot enough, or else it was too hot and I burned the bread. I was forever letting the fire go out. We had a load of coal hauled out from Chugwater. I washed the dishes in a minimum of water. That water was saved and used again. I rinsed the dishes and used the water to wash out a few clothes or scrub the floor. The pan of water that we used to wash our hands was never thrown out until it was really dirty. I did laundry with that detested washboard, and never had half enough water to suit me!

Earle used the sled to bring barrels of water from the Casters' well. Usually he was able to get home with half a barrelful after bumping over the prairie. We had a well-worn trail between our place and Casters' place before very long. There was nothing more we could do at our place. Luther was building a fence to keep stock in for the winter, and Earle helped with that. Then there was a shed to build for Luther, more daylong trips to Chugwater for materials: lumber, barbed wire, and fence posts. Twenty miles each way with a load coming back. The men were gone from dawn till dark.

Cecil and Wayne were a great help, and Osa was a good little housekeeper. Mrs. Caster was busy constantly. She put up a clothesline, but found that mere clothespins could not withstand the wind and keep the clothes on the line. So she had to hang everything up on barbed-wire fences around the yard.

We talked it over and decided that we'd made a mistake when we located our house. For many miles to the north was state land leased by the McDonald ranch, which could not be homesteaded, so there was no hope of new neighbors in that direction. During the summer and fall, every good half-section to the west and south had been filed on. The families would be coming out in the spring.

Our land sloped uphill to the south. The southwest corner was the perfect place for a house. We could see across the valley more than twenty miles to the south. Laramie Range was in view to the west and Laramie Peak to the north. If we moved our house, we would be near neighbors and could see other houses once they were built.

Under the homesteading regulations, we had to establish residence within six months of filing—and then live on our claim for not less than seven months out of the year for three years. We also had to have forty acres under cultivation. We had established our residence and built our house. There was absolutely nothing else we could do until spring. Besides, Earle felt he should be earning money instead of just spending it. We knew we had to squeeze every penny to keep us going for three years and make the necessary improvements on the claim.

The evenings were long. We just sat there and looked at each other. Every week Earle rode to Diamond to get the mail on the day *The Saturday Evening Post* arrived. We couldn't afford any other magazines, so we read *The Saturday Evening Post* from cover to cover. There was a serial entitled "Within the Law." I always read that aloud the first thing. Then we took turns reading the rest of the magazine.[1]

We had complained to the Casters about having nothing to read. "I've got some books," Luther said. "Just wait till our goods get here and you can borrow them." At last the books were unpacked and Luther handed them over proudly. He had two books by Mrs. E. D. E. N. Southworth, titled *In the Depths* and *Out of the Depths*. That was all. I have read better books.[2]

Dr. William R. Day delighted us all by coming out and looking for a claim. He had a good practice in the town of Moravia, but it was a night-and-day business in all kinds of weather. He had lived right across the street from us in Moravia, and was quite wealthy. He was a very handsome, gray-haired man, always very carefully dressed. He never went anywhere without putting on his gloves. Dr. Day had told Earle, "You know, I'm tired of this mud and country driving. I'd like to take a claim, too. I'd just like to 'rusticate' for a few years," he explained to us. "People telephone me in the middle of the night. I have to call the boy to hitch up the team and drive five or six miles in the mud or snow. If they had to come after me, they'd wait till morning. Here, there's no telephones. And this soil isn't bottomless mud in rainy weather like we've got in southern Iowa."

---

1   Unfortunately, I was not able to find a serial with this title in *The Saturday Evening Post* in either 1913 or 1914. It may be that Laura gives an incorrect title, as she does for the Southworth books in the subsequent paragraph.

2   Emma Dorothy Eliza Nevitte Southworth was one of the most popular novelists of the late nineteenth century. Smith is probably referring to *Ishmael; or In the Depths* (Philadelphia: T. B. Peterson, 1876) and *Self-Raised; or From the Depths* (Philadelphia: T. B. Peterson, 1876). One critic describes *Ishmael* as a bestseller on the order of *Uncle Tom's Cabin*. Southworth's novels were generally uplifting stories of good versus evil. Laura's quip suggests that this kind of moralism may have been somewhat dated by the early twentieth century (Mary Noel, *Villains Galore: The Heyday of the Popular Story Weekly*, New York: Macmillan, 1954, 161–165; Nina Baym, *Woman's Fiction: A Guide to Novels By and About Women in America, 1820–1870*, Ithaca: Cornell, 1978, 110–118).

All of us were anxious to have the doctor take a claim near us, but all the land in the vicinity had been filed on. There wasn't a doctor closer than Cheyenne, fifty miles away. Most of the people who were filing claims hereabout had been Dr. Day's patients in Moravia. It seemed to me that things would be much improved if we had a doctor nearby.

Luther hitched up his light team to the surrey and set off with Earle and Dr. Day early the next morning on their quest for land. The day was interminable; hour after hour dragged by. The screaming wind dashed sand against the window endlessly. By late afternoon they still had not returned. I had never stayed alone in the cabin at night, and I began to become frightened. They might have decided to stay overnight in some other homestead. But then again, they might have gotten lost. I thought of all the terrible things that could go wrong.

The Casters' house was a mile away up over the hill, where I couldn't even see their light. There wasn't a house for miles in any other direction. The wind blew harder and louder than usual. Every few minutes, I went out to the door to look for the men. As dusk approached, I became even more frightened.

It was nearly dark when I panicked. I could not stand it any longer! I put on my coat and scarf, blew out the light, closed up the house, and started to run toward Casters' house. The trail went up a long hill, and I was soon out of breath. I slowed to a trot—and then I heard the coyotes. Then I really ran! I tripped on a stone and fell, sure that the beasts would pounce on me. It seemed to me that the coyotes were closing in on me from every direction. I scrambled to my feet and stumbled on up the hill. At last I could see lights at the Casters' house! I slowed up, but I was still panting when I knocked on their door. Ethel looked at me in astonishment.

"You've torn your dress," she said, scowling gently. "You shouldn't be out after dark alone."

"The men haven't come home. I was afraid to stay alone," I explained. Already I felt silly. Their house was snug and warm. The smell of fresh bread was delicious. The lamp burned brightly on the table. I was ashamed of myself. I realized I had been silly.

The men came home within an hour. Earle was annoyed because I hadn't stayed home and had a light on for him. They'd tried to find our house, but couldn't see it in the dark. So Luther had done the only possible thing and gave the horses their heads. They found their way home. Dr. Day decided that he wanted to file on a claim, but they had not been able to find any good land still open.

Maudy Buckmaster was a young bachelor who had filed a claim, but he'd had enough of loneliness in the few months he'd been here. He had no capital to develop his claim, and there was no work to be had in the vicinity. He filed a notice of relinquishment, and Dr. Day filed on his claim. That was perfect for us. The claim lay to the west of us—the shack where we had first stayed. It was just north of the Casters', so we would have near neighbors and the wonderful comfort of a good physician right at hand. We had lived just across the street from Dr. Day and his wife Jessie in Moravia, and were very fond of them both. Mrs. Day was rather chunky and short. They had no children. We were so much younger than them, they said Earle and I were almost like their relatives.[3]

---

3   The Days took up the north half of section 22, so they were directly west of the Smiths and north of the Casters.

Chapter Nine

Mellie Baker

I HAD JUST FINISHED MY MORNING WORK ONE DAY WHEN WE HEARD a wagon drive up and stop in front of our house. Someone yelled "Smith!", so we went out.

"My name is Baker," the guy said. "Got a claim over here, and I need some help to get my fence in. Like to have you both come over and help for a couple of days." He was a rough-looking chap, gaunt and grizzled, his face burned brown from the wind and sun. He was definitely not prepossessing. He wore a ragged shirt and not-too-clean bib overalls. He had a sorry-looking team with a patched harness and an old wagon. He also had a couple of kids.

"Mellie here, she's only fourteen, and she kinda needs a lift. Jim, he's sixteen, and he's pretty good help. But I do need another man on that fencing job."

"Well," Earle said reluctantly, "we can come over for a couple days."

"When you need some help I'll come over and pay you back," Baker offered.

All we had to do was close the padlock on the door and we were ready to leave. Earle saddled our horse and I climbed into the wagon. The spring seat had no back, and I nearly went over backwards before I noticed it. Baker motioned with his thumb, and the two youngsters sat on the floor in the back of the wagon. It was seven or eight miles to his claim. He'd built a stable, and the family lived in one end of it while the horses, cows, and a few chickens lived in the other end.

"Won't bother to unhitch the team. Might as well get to working on that fence," he said gruffly. "Take you girls about an hour to get dinner, I suppose." There were the inevitable navy beans soaking on the back of the stove.

"I'll build up the fire," Mellie said, "and we'll cook some potatoes. Can you bake biscuits, Mrs. Smith? Pa says my biscuits are like rocks, and he gets awful mad."

"Yes, I can make biscuits," I said. "Let's have some fried potatoes, too. Those beans will cook pretty quick since they've been soaking."

"This morning's milk is sweet, and we've got butter. It ain't very good. I can't seem to make it like Ma did," Mellie explained. "Can't make anything as good as she did. Ma died a year ago. I work all the time and still I don't get nothin' done." Mellie was a large girl for her age, and Jim was tall and husky for sixteen. Both were sullen and quiet.

We had dinner ready when the men came in. The one room was crowded with a stove, a table, a few chairs, and a bed. It was hot. The double bed was pushed against the wall in one corner, the kitchen cabinet crowded beside the stove. A pile of dirty clothing was heaped in another corner, and over everything was the smell of the horses, cows, and chickens that were on the other side of the board partition.

We would have to use the haymow to dress and undress. Earle would sleep with Baker in the loft and I would share the bed with Mellie.

Baker had no time to talk during the meal, or to pass anything to others. He was too busy shoveling the food in with his knife. The table was small, so everyone just helped themselves.

Baker shoved back his chair. "Jim, you bring in some water and put it on the stove. Carry in some more wood; there's a heap of washin' to do." He looked directly at Mellie, but there was a side glance for me, too. Right then I figured that I wasn't gonna wash filthy overalls on a washboard for anybody. I had plenty of that kind of work at home.

"Come on," he grunted. "Gotta get that fence done so's the stock'll have more feed." And he was out the door. Jim silently went to get the wood and water from the well and windmill. Earle finished his dinner and followed them out.

"Mellie," I offered, "I'll wash the dishes if you want to get at your washing. Then if you have any mending, I can do that."

"I think that's why Ma died," Mellie said bitterly. "Pa made her work all the time. I don't want you to help with the washing, but there's a lot of clothes need mending. I just can't sew."

She started to get the soiled clothes together, and then asked eagerly, "Mrs. Smith, could you make some pies while we've got the stove going? We got some dried peaches."

"Of course I can, Mellie," I said. "Let's put the peaches on the back of the stove to cook slowly for a while; then I'll bake a couple pies so we can have some for supper. If you have any cream ready to churn, I'll do that, and show you how to wash the butter so it won't be milky."

We were busy all afternoon. They had a small churn, which sadly needed scalding. That done, I made butter. I washed it thoroughly in the cold well water and salted it. Mellie thought she could do it after watching me.

She found an old pair of overalls past mending, and I cut them up to make patches for the denim overalls and denim jackets. It seemed that everything needed mending. There was no sewing machine, so I had to do it all by hand. It was a slow job. Mellie rubbed and scrubbed most of the afternoon. Her face became more weary and sullen as time passed. I hung the clothes on the barbed-wire fence around the house for her. They dried fast in the whistling wind.

She brightened up when I made the pies. I made a small one in a saucer for her, which I made her eat with a glass of milk as soon as it was cool. "Ma used to make little pies for me," she said huskily. She looked outside to be sure her father was not in sight before she ate it. Then she carefully washed the saucer and put it away.

The men worked till nearly dark on the fence. Baker asked, "Can you milk a cow, Smith?"

"Nope," Earle lied cheerfully. "Never milked a cow in my life."

Baker grunted, took the pail, and milked the cow. We had the same menu for supper: potatoes, boiled beans, and hot biscuits. But we boiled the potatoes and I made gravy the way Ethel Caster had showed me, only I browned some butter and then added flour and milk.

Mellie ventured to ask her father, "Ain't this gravy good, Pa?"

"Yep," he answered.

Just from habit, I cut the pie in six pieces before putting it on the table. "Did you use all them peaches, Mellie?" Baker demanded angrily.

I cut in quickly, "Oh no. It doesn't take very many dried peaches to make a pie."

Each of us had a piece of pie. Baker downed his and then reached for the extra piece without the faintest hesitation. Mellie was sitting next to me. She nudged my knee. We had hidden the second pie.

After supper, while she and I washed the dishes, the men sat and talked. Earle and Jim were too tired to talk much, but Baker gloried in having a new audience. He reeled off one tall tale after another in which he was invariably the hero. And each time the story ended up with "You mebbe won't believe it, but them's the facts."

The men climbed the ladder to the hayloft. Mellie and I fell into bed. There were three hens roosting on top of the partition. They could've been roosting on the bed and it wouldn't have bothered me. I was too tired to be bothered by the horses, the cows, the chickens, or anything on the other side of the partition. I was asleep instantly.

I couldn't believe it was morning when I heard Baker rattling the stove lids, making the fire, and ordering us all to get up. The sun hadn't even thought of rising yet. We cooked oatmeal for breakfast, and more biscuits. Before he went outdoors, Jim asked hesitantly if we could have more gravy for breakfast, so I made a big bowl of the same gravy we'd had the night before.

"Did you get the washin' done, Mellie?" Baker asked harshly.

"Most of it," she answered sulkily.

"Get it done this morning!" he ordered. "Looks like rain." There wasn't a cloud in the sky, but Mellie carried in more water and rubbed and scrubbed again, while I mended the clothes that she'd washed the day before.

Dinner was the same: potatoes, gravy, boiled beans, and biscuits. This time I cut the pie in five pieces so Baker couldn't get any more than the rest of us. Mellie poked my knee and I almost giggled. Earle sat on my other side. As we finished dinner, I poked him with my foot and said, "You know, Earle, we'll have to get home this afternoon. You promised Luther Caster you would help him tomorrow."

Earle looked straight at me. He didn't even blink. "That's right—tomorrow's Thursday. Well, I'll work a while, Baker, until I help you get that corner braced. And then we'll head home."

Baker blustered, "Don't see how I can hitch up and take you home today. Tomorrow'd do just as well. What's yer hurry?"

To Baker's evident chagrin, Earle replied, "Oh, that's all right. We've ridden our horse double before. We'll just go on home today. Let's get that corner done before we go."

"I wished you'd stay," Mellie said wistfully.

"Shet up," Baker said sharply. "Mrs. Smith couldn't learn you nothin' if she stayed a month."

"Won't need any help this fall, will ya, Mr. Smith?" Baker continued. "Got so much work myself before winter sets in, I can't get it all done. Come spring, you just let me know, and Jim and me will come over and help ya."

We both knew that Baker had no intention of ever paying back Earle's work, and even the thought of having him around was distasteful. We were weary of "Mebbe you won't believe it, but them's the facts."[1]

"No," Earle answered. "I've done all I can on my place this fall."

Mellie and I worked until she finished the washing and I completed the mending. Earle came back to the house—or rather, the stable—in the middle of the afternoon. He saddled the horse and boosted me up.

"Come over and see me sometime, Mellie," I said. I felt terribly sorry for the child. Even though she was much taller than I was, she was still a child.

She shook her head and said sadly, "I don't think Pa will let me. He's mad 'cause you won't stay."

Earle climbed up behind the saddle and we set off in the general direction of home. I sat swaying in the saddle as the horse plodded along through the grass. It was such a nice word, *home*. It was unquestionably as humble as it could be, but it was *our* home, our safe haven. We could get there before dark, even though the horse walked. As we rode over a rise, the Bakers' place was out of sight. There was nothing in any direction but the brown buffalo grass swaying under the rule of the west wind blowing over the rolling land. It was suddenly a very lonely day.

Presently I snapped out, "That old coot! The idea of him thinking he could fool us into working like a couple of mules for just as long as he wanted us to! He even thought I was gonna help with the washing!" I was so angry I could hardly keep still.

"We certainly earned our bed and board," Earle said gloomily. "I've never slept in a haymow before. It's pretty scratchy. What are we gonna have for supper—beans?"

---

1   The idea of work exchange was widespread in the rural West. Work was expected to be returned in kind, and some families even kept account books of the hours of work they owed their neighbors and that were owed to them. See Mary Neth, *Preserving the Family Farm: Women, Community, and the Foundations of Agribusiness in the Midwest, 1900–1940* (Baltimore: Johns Hopkins, 1995), 54–59.

"No sir!" I said decidedly. "We are going to have ham and potatoes and gravy. I'm going to open a can of tomatoes and one of peaches, and we'll have biscuits."

"That sounds good. I'm hungry right now," he said enthusiastically.

"There surely won't be many more people like Baker up here," I said hopefully. "We know the Casters are real people, and Dr. and Mrs. Day will be out in the spring. I hope we never see any of the Bakers again!"[2]

"Did you notice his face when I said we could ride double?" Earle went on. "He thought we'd have to stay until he was good and ready to take us home. Another thing that got under my skin—every once in a while he would call me 'Professor.' You know how I detest that. After living all my life in a college town, and knowing so many real professors, being called 'Professor' myself just because I was principal of a school always seemed utterly silly."

We both began to laugh. We laughed until we were weak. I hung onto the pommel of the saddle to keep from falling off. Earle got off the horse and walked most of the way home, even though he was tired. It was easier than riding behind the saddle with his legs dangling. Two hours later we were home.

"I hope there's enough water to last till morning," Earle said wearily. "I don't feel like walking another two miles."

"There's a pail half full; we'll make do," I replied. "I know you're tired."

The next day we told Casters about our visit to the Bakers', and Luther said, "I heard they were coming out here. I'm afraid they won't make many friends if they treat everybody like that. Baker's neighbors in Iowa didn't have much to say for him, but I never knew him personally."

---

2   From what I can tell, there were no Bakers living in the area when the US Census was taken in 1920; however, since Laura fails to give Mr. Baker's first name, it is difficult to determine conclusively. Of course, the Smiths were also no longer in Wyoming in 1920.

One day while Earle was gone, some men stopped by to see me about the horse, Dick. They said Jim Dawson had never paid for the horse, and they'd come to take him back. I didn't know what to do. The loss of our horse was a terrible blow. I can see why they always hanged horse thieves in the West. Without a horse, a man was helpless on the prairie. When Earle got home he was upset.

"Why did you let them take him?" Earle asked.

"What could I do?" I said. "I didn't have any bill of sale, and after Claude Long's deal with Jim Dawson, when Jim didn't pay for his board, I figured that he very likely didn't pay for the horse either. I had no choice," I explained despondently.

"That settles it," said Earle. "We can't get along without a horse! I'm going to write the teachers to get a job teaching in Iowa this winter. Luther wants me to go to Chugwater with him tomorrow, so I'll mail the letter then."

"And I'll go to California and stay with Mother and Sis. I have a standing invitation there." Then I thought of something else, "Why, Earle—you'll have to carry water again! We can't even use the barrel on the sled without a horse."

So we decided to leave for the winter. Earle wrote that night to apply for the job. I wrote Mother that I might come out, knowing that I would get an immediate reply, urging me to come. I was still the baby of the family.

Wagon with wood from the foothills. LAURA GIBSON SMITH PAPERS, IOWA WOMEN'S ARCHIVES, UNIVERSITY OF IOWA LIBRARIES

CHAPTER TEN

Snow

WE HAD A BEAUTIFUL AUTUMN. THE WIND BLEW CONSTANTLY, BUT WE learned to fasten everything down or else chase it a mile. The days were pleasant, though the nights were cold. We had some rain, which meant a few pails of lovely soft water. I had pails and kettles under every dribble along the eaves when it rained.

There was nothing to do on the homestead until spring. Earle had gotten the school job in Iowa, and my mother invited me to spend the winter with her in southern California. We were very conscientious about living the required time on the claim, so we planned to stay until December.

In November, Luther Caster made his plans for the winter. None of us had any idea what winter might be like in Wyoming. Luther, Earle, and the two older boys planned to take two wagons up to the foothills to gather wood. Then after resting the horses for a day, they would take the wagons to Chugwater for coal and groceries.

They left at daylight to gather the wood. That was one of the kind things that the ranchers did for us settlers: They let the homesteaders go through their land up to the foothills to cut all the dead trees they wanted. Cecil and Wayne Caster considered this to be quite a lark, and they did their full share of the work.

It was over twenty miles to the spot where they planned to gather wood, so the men took food and blankets and slept in the wagon that night. They gathered the wood and returned the second day, arriving home at dusk, weary and dirty, but with the wagon loaded high with good pitch pine.

The morning the men planned to go to Chugwater to get groceries and coal, we were up early. There was snow on the ground and it was still coming down. It was hardly falling; it just drifted down gently and settled as though weary. There was no wind.

"I don't like the looks of this snow," Earle said, worried. "I'm going over to Casters' and tell Luther we'd better put off the trip to Chugwater for a day or two. I was caught in a blizzard when I first came out last March, and I don't want to be caught out on the open prairie for another one."

"You'd better come right back," I admonished. "There's no telling when it will start snowing hard."

It snowed all day. All night, it snowed. Earle opened our door frequently and swept it off for fear that we would not be able to lift it with the weight of the snow. It continued snowing for seven days and seven nights. It was not a roaring blizzard with bitter cold and driving wind; it was simply a snowstorm piling up as though it would never stop. There was some wind at night.[1]

Earle made a pair of snowshoes from the side boards of the apple box by cutting off angles to make an unreasonable [*sic*] facsimile of real snowshoes. He bored holes in them and tied them on his feet with binder twine. He wandered around near our house to try them out, and then struck off up the hill to Casters'. The south gable of our cabin was free of snow, and it showed as a good landmark amid the great expanse of white. He could use it to find his way home. Coming back, he saw a jackrabbit floundering in the deep snow. He hustled into the house for the rifle and took a couple shots at it, but missed. So he ran it down. I stewed the rabbit and baked it in the oven. It was very good for a change.

1   Chugwater weather records for December 1–5, 1913, record five consecutive days of snow totaling twenty-four inches (NOAA / National Weather Service preliminary data; Barbara Mayes Boustead, NOAA, e-mail message to author, September 23, 2010).

Although we could not get to Chugwater, we didn't have to worry about food or fuel for ourselves. We had bought six big, young roosters, each weighing about six pounds. We became tired of chicken each time I cooked one, but it was a change from ham and salmon. There was no refrigeration in those days, so I had to cook the whole chicken at once. There was plenty of water; I kept pans of snow melting on the stove all the time.

When the storm was over and the sun came out, we pushed our door open and stood blinking at the dazzling white like a couple of prairie dogs. There was two feet of snow on the level ground and up to twenty feet in the draws. But on the top of the hill toward Casters', there was only six inches. The wind had leveled everything into one vast sameness. The hills and gullies had vanished. Our little pond had frozen and was covered deep with snow. There was no indication where the snow was deep or shallow. All the fences had disappeared; not even a post showed. In every direction, there was nothing but the white undulating expanse of snow stretching to the far hills.

Now it was a question of how to get to the train at Diamond. Earle bundled up in his sheepskin coat, tied on the makeshift snowshoes, and went up to Casters'. I wanted to try snowshoes, too, but we had no more boards.

"This is the problem," Earle told them. "I have to teach school in Iowa, and I've got to start back pretty soon or I won't be there when the term begins. I have to get to Cheyenne somehow."

"I don't think the horses could get through even to Diamond now," Luther said.

Earle agreed. "I've been doing pretty well in these snowshoes I've fixed up. I think I can get to Diamond on them. It's only about five miles. I can stay up on the dry land until that last draw that leads down to the bridge over Chugwater Creek."

"I've been making a bobsled. When the snow settles, we could bring Laura to Diamond," Luther offered. "I have to go anyway."

Earle came home and told me his arrangements. We packed his suitcase that afternoon. He left the next morning about ten o'clock, which gave him plenty of time to get to the train by four. He was dressed warmly in a heavy coat, fur cap, and overshoes, with his trousers tied down inside the overshoes. I stood at the door and watched as he made fairly good progress across the little valley and up the long hill, becoming a black speck finally. Then he was out of sight.

It was a good five miles he would have to take to avoid the gullies where he knew there'd be deep drifts. He plodded along for perhaps two miles, resting occasionally, shifting the suitcase from one hand to the other as his fingers grew numb from the weight and cold. He felt encouraged with his progress—until the string broke on one of the snowshoes. He had more twine in his pocket for just such an emergency, and had put a large nail in the suitcase to poke frozen snow out of the holes. He opened the suitcase and pawed into the corners, but he could not find the nail. He felt for his pocketknife and realized that he'd left it on the table at home. He had nothing to push the snow out of the holes so that he could put on the new twine. He searched through the suitcase again, but could not find the nail. There was no choice but to leave the snowshoes and go on as best he could.

The snow was three feet deep. The going was hard. Every step he took, he sank into the soft snow over his knees. He wallowed through snow nearly up to his waist for some distance, and then suddenly went in up to his armpits. He dragged himself out by putting both arms up over the suitcase. Then he swung the suitcase and dragged himself to it again. Over and over he had to go through this maneuver until he reached high ground where he could touch solid earth again. It was impossible to tell where the gullies were. The wind had drifted the snow so smooth that it all looked alike.

By that time it was well after noon. He struggled along, pulling one foot out of the snow, stepping into more snow above his knees, then repeating the process with the other foot. Several more times he stepped off into gullies, and each time he had to use the suitcase to drag himself out. Late afternoon came, and finally dusk. He heard the train whistle in Diamond; heard it stop and go on again. It was after four o'clock.

As the daylight faded, he saw coyotes slinking soundlessly along, keeping pace with him a few rods away on each side. He knew they would not attack him. He yelled at them and they trotted off a short distance and sat on their haunches. When he started on again, the sinister beasts again kept pace along either side.

Another light gleamed as the bright moon rose. At last he could be sure of his directions. Earle floundered along, now again in deep snow. He recognized the draw that led down to the bridge. The snow might be deeper still, but he had to keep going. He reached the bottom of the draw and found the bridge over the creek. He was soon on the railroad track, where the snow was only rail-deep. The coyotes raised their unholy clamor at the moon. After all the exertion, Earle wasn't even cold. He walked briskly down the track to the station and rapped on the door.

"How did you get here?" asked Mr. Lingwall in amazement.

"I walked in from the claim," Earle said, grinning. It had taken him over seven hours to get there.

While finishing his hot supper of ham and eggs, Earle's feet began to feel hot and swollen. He took off his shoes and socks and found that both feet had frostbite. Mrs. Lingwall put kerosene on them and rubbed them with snow.[2] The following day his feet were so swollen that he had to wear bedroom slippers on the train to Cheyenne.

That afternoon Luther brought Osa down to stay with me. Mrs. Caster wouldn't think of letting me stay alone. The two older boys, Cecil and Wayne, rode one of the heavy team horses, and Luther with Osa behind him rode the other.

---

2   "Frostbite Treatment with Kerosene: Massage kerosene on the affected parts. Kerosene has long been used to treat many different injuries." See Jude C. Todd, *Jude's Herbal Home Remedies: Natural Health, Beauty & Home-Care Secrets,* 2nd ed. (St. Paul: Llewellyn Publications, 2004), 99.

"Pretty hard going in all of this snow," he said. "It'll be a few days before we can take you to Diamond, Laura."

"Any time will suit me," I assured him. "I have plenty of food and can melt snow for water. The snow ought to settle in a few days. Or maybe we'll have one of those chinook winds come along and melt it in a hurry."

"It's getting colder all the time. Are you sure you have enough coal and everything?" He was worried. I assured him that Osa and I would get along just fine. We agreed that there was no lack of snow to melt for water.

It grew dark early. Osa and I had our supper and settled ourselves for the evening. We were startled to hear a man shouting. Neither of us was really frightened, but I said, "We'll both show ourselves at the door, Osa."

We pushed up the outside door and gave an answering yell. We saw one of the neighbors from a few miles east come riding toward us through the snow. He had been hunting wolves on horseback and gotten lost. We told him whose place he had found and pointed the way home. Osa and I latched the doors very carefully as we went back inside to the warmth and cheer of the little room.

"I'm glad it wasn't a stranger," I said. "And I'm glad you're here, Osa."

— ᴗ —

Several days later, Luther decided he had to go to town for flour and other groceries, and would have to make a road. He could take the train from Diamond to Chugwater and be back in the afternoon. Luther and the boys came down in bobsleds and hauled all my groceries and the two remaining roosters up to their house. Then they came back for Osa and me. I felt no regret emptying every drop of water and closing the little cabin tight against the winter cold. I was ready to leave.

The following morning Luther hitched the light team to his homemade bobsled, which consisted only of runners and cross braces, with two boards nailed across the top. We tied on a barrel, made some handholds of rope, and were ready. Cecil and Wayne each rode one of the heavy horses and went ahead of us to break a trail. Luther hitched the light team to the sled.

Mrs. Caster knew it would be a long, lonely winter for them, but she smiled cheerfully as she said to me, "We'll see you in the spring, Laura."

The snow was up to the bellies of the horses. We went slowly through the gate a half-mile away and into McDonald's pasture. We got along without any real trouble. It was hard going for the horses up the long hill to the higher land.

"Swing out farther to the right," Luther shouted to the boys. "We'll hit gullies if you stay too close to the rim of the draw."

"Strange how the wind blew the snow and smoothed out every rough spot," I said. "It all looks as smooth as a tabletop in every direction."

"Yes, but we come this way when we go to gather wood. I know the area. We're going to have to go a little to the east, or we'll be in some deep spots for sure!" Luther explained. We went a little farther and stopped to rest the horses. Even the two horses the boys rode were puffing.

We hit some rocks and tipped this way and that. I fell off the barrel sled, climbed on again, secured a better hold, and off we went. Several times the horses ahead sank in the snow up to their bellies. Luther would swing out a little farther so we would miss the gully. We plodded along, fighting the snow foot by foot, rod by rod, for mile after mile. Cecil was ten years old, and Wayne was nine, but they were fully capable of handling their part of the journey. In the broad daylight, Luther had no difficulty in finding the way down to the draw which led to the bridge over Chugwater Creek.

It took us over four hours to make the trip of about five miles. All of us were glad to get there. Luther took my trunk off the sled. It was battered and scraped beyond any further use. Luther and the boys stayed only a little while to get warm, rest the horses, and get the mail.

"It won't be so bad going back," Luther said. "We can follow our tracks. The trail will be easier for the horses. Ethel is going to worry until we get home, so we'd better be off."

The Lingwalls and I watched as they crossed the bridge and plodded around the bend into the draw.

"They are wonderful people," I said. "I don't believe I could have stuck it out this fall if they hadn't come. With six children they leave a settled community and take a claim out here. I honestly feel ashamed to go away and leave Mrs. Caster without another woman near, but Earle felt he had to make some money this winter—and there isn't one blessed thing we can do on the homestead until spring."[3]

"Don't you worry, Mrs. Smith," Mr. Lingwall replied. "With those two boys, Luther will make out. I've seen them when they went through here going after wood, and I tell you, they are a couple of men right now."

Many weeks would pass before the snow finally melted. Luther drove to Diamond to take the morning train into Chugwater and returned that afternoon with groceries and supplies.

Earle was still in Cheyenne when I arrived. His frozen feet were still painful and swollen, but he didn't lose any toes. I thought I had survived a hard journey through the snow, but when Earle told me about his experiences, I had to agree that they were much worse. He had finally found that all-important nail in a pocket of his suitcase. He had certainly put it in a safe place—even if he couldn't find it when he needed it to dig the snow and ice out of the holes in his snowshoes!

---

3   It is unlikely that the Smiths had spent a great deal of the inheritance and therefore were in desperate need of funds. I believe that they were willing to spend the inheritance money on major projects (including building a house and drilling a well the next summer) but they wanted to keep money coming in for ongoing expenses.

Chapter Eleven

Spring 1914

When we returned to Diamond in the spring, everything *was* different. Instead of bare trees along the creek, now there were fresh green leaves. The magpies called raucously to each other as they flirted through the bushes. The prairie was a rolling green, with wildflowers blooming everywhere. A lark bunting, with smart white on his wings, warbled as he mounted into the sky. The field sparrows sang and the meadowlarks trilled from sagebrush and fence posts. Everything was bursting with the miracle of spring, and we felt real elation. Where we had felt only bewilderment and uncertainty in the fall, now we could see what we had to do—and in some manner, how we were going to accomplish it.

The wary white-faced cows with their awkward calves kept watch as we drove through McDonald's pasture. We knew we had our little house waiting for us, although when we got there we found it had been broken into and all the blankets, as well as Earle's cherished sheepskin coat, were gone.

With a supply of groceries purchased in Cheyenne, I was ready for anything. I had several loaves of bread, yeast, baking powder, and soda. I had bought dried fruit and canned vegetables, bacon and ham, eggs and butter, as well as potatoes and flour.

But there was the old problem of water until we could drill a well, and that would have to wait until we built our new home up on the hilltop. More important things had to come first.

Other families who had filed the previous fall had arrived while we were gone and put up their small houses. A dwelling on every half-section made a very different picture from the utterly uninhabited landscape we had seen with such dismay when we first came.

Dr. and Mrs. Day had arrived and were living in the Buckmaster shack while building their house. They had shipped out a freight-car load of furniture and equipment. They brought three driving horses and a Jersey milk cow. We arranged to have them include our few crates of furniture and books with their belongings. Earle bought one of Dr. Day's horses, Bill, so we were no longer afoot. At least Earle wasn't.

Dr. Day and his wife were building their house directly across the road from where we intended to build ours, so there would be four houses about a quarter of a mile apart on the respective corners of the half-sections. The doctor had his well drilled, and that solved our immediate problem of water. It was much closer than the Casters' well. Earle fixed up his sled built of fence posts, fastened on the barrel again, and hauled water day after day from Dr. Day's well. The prairie had not changed in roughness, so Earle was fortunate to get home with a half-barrel of water. He always thought I was terribly extravagant in my use of it.

To the south of us, Dave Gillaspie had located on his homestead. He was a widower of many years, with extremely lax ideas of house-keeping. He built a small two-room shack, where he lived in one room and kept his team of horses in the other room. He was a stooped, old man with grizzled hair and unshaven face. He wore a greasy cap winter and summer. His clothes were always dirty. In the cold weather he wore felt boots—something I hadn't seen since my early childhood when my father wore them with overshoes in extremely cold weather on the farm.

Dave came down one evening to talk about the fencing between our land and his. The fence would have to run for a mile east and west. The men agreed that each one would fence half of it, as was the custom. Earle wanted to be certain that our field of grain was tightly fenced, so he offered to fence the east half-mile, and Dave could fence the remaining half-mile to the west. That suited Dave, and it was thus agreed.

Dave happened to see a gallon of corn syrup on the cupboard. "Mrs. Smith, do you like sorghum 'lasses?"

I said, "Yes, very much. But it's been years since I've had any real sorghum."

"Well, I got a gallon of sorghum 'lasses that I'll trade you for that there corn syrup," he offered.

"That's a deal!" I said. "You bring it down anytime and you can have the corn syrup."

Dave didn't stay very long. He chewed tobacco constantly, and he couldn't find any place to spit in my house. He looked at the stove, but that clean gray enamel daunted him. The coal bucket was much too far from him, and the woodbox was under the reservoir of the stove. Every time he got desperate to spit, he had to open the door, climb the stairs, and spit on the ground. It was far too much effort, so he stayed only a short time after they'd agreed on the fencing.

A few days later, I had just finished the supper dishes and stepped around the corner of the house to throw out the dishwater. I gave it a good hearty fling and caught old Dave square in the face with it as he came around the corner of the house. He sputtered and fumed while I tried to convince him that I hadn't seen him coming. I think he would have left if he hadn't wanted that corn syrup so badly. He came in and we made the trade for the sorghum molasses, but I believe he always did think I doused him purposely with that pan of soapy dishwater.

Dave didn't build much of a fence, so we were very glad that we had arranged to take the east half along our field.

Dave never knew it, but Teddy Roosevelt was responsible for his fence. In Wyoming and the other Western states, the ranchers had bought or filed on huge tracts of land under the first Homestead Act of 1862. They found that by building their fences from one homestead to the next, they could enclose vast acreages of public land which could not be reached by anyone else. The ranchers could then use it for their own herds without actual ownership.

When President Roosevelt came to office, he ordered maps prepared showing such fences, the areas enclosed by which gave illegal use of the land. He ordered the cavalry deployed armed with wire cutters. They rode through the prairie, and wherever they found an illegal fence according to their maps, they dismounted and cut the barbed wire between every two posts. Then they'd mount and ride on to the next fence. Fences that legally bounded the ranchers' property were left intact.

It was in one of those vast acreages opened up for homesteads that we had our claim. The ranchers had salvaged most of the fence posts, but old Dave drove hither and yon, gathering up rusted lengths of barbed wire for his fence. He seldom found a piece more than twenty feet long, but he patiently spliced the wire together and built sort of a fence. His horses were old and were satisfied with the grass at home, but our cows hardly hesitated if they took a notion to go through Old Dave's fence.

There was one other family in the vicinity who afforded the neighbors almost as much amusement as we did with our ignorance of the simplest things. Mr. Whittle had been a coal miner in southern Iowa, and had even less experience with farms and farm animals than we had. His family had a claim some eight or ten miles from us. Someone in Iowa had finagled him into buying a beautiful team of draft mares, with the idea that he could raise better horses than the light western horses and make money on them. One of these mares turned out to be a jumper, and would go over any fence in the district. She constantly jumped into the grain fields and kept us busy chasing her home lest she founder on the unripe grain.[1]

The first time I saw Mrs. Whittle was after we had moved into our new house. She came driving into our yard with this beautiful team hitched to a lumber wagon, and brought me a heaping panful of mushrooms.

"They look wonderful, Mrs. Whittle," I said as I thanked her. "But you'll have to tell me how to cook them. I've never cooked mushrooms."

She had a very broad English accent, and I could scarcely understand her. "You just cut them up and fry them in butter or drippings. I'm on my way to Diamond to get the mail; shall I get yours, too?"

"Yes, thank you. Earle has been too busy to go for several days. We would appreciate that, but can't you sit down a little while and talk?"

"No, I have to get home," she said. I emptied the mushrooms from the pan and away she went. She trotted the horses out onto the road, then gave them a slap with the reins and galloped them down the hill. I watched in horror, fully expecting one of them to stumble, but they made it safely, She had to pull them up to stop at the gate half a mile away.

A couple of hours later she drove back to bring me the mail. She let the horses walk up the hill and then urged them into a gallop. Down the hill they went away to the south, the wagon bounding with every jump. All of the neighbors worried about her driving, but she never did have an accident.

---

1   James Whittle and his wife Mary were both born in England, he around 1870 and she around 1880. They had seven children in 1920: Bertha (twenty), Ada (fifteen), Doris (thirteen), David (eleven), Albert (eight), Mary (five), and Leona (two). He also appears in an accounts receivable ledger for the Swan Mercantile Store in Chugwater in 1914, owing $16.15 (1920 US Census, www.ancestry.com, accessed August 10, 2010; "Accounts Receivable—Swan Mercantile Store, Chugwater, Wyoming, Nov. 30, 1914," Box 29, Folder 8, Swan Company Records, 1877–1984, Collection 11470, American Heritage Center, University of Wyoming, Laramie, Wyoming).

The Whittles had six children, and not too much capital, so Mr. Whittle was away working most of the time while the family lived on the claim. Mrs. Whittle was fully capable of doing any of the work that needed to be done.

Elvy Gillaspie filed on a claim a couple of miles south of us. Elvy was Dave Gillaspie's son. He drove from Nebraska with a team and lumber wagon, bringing his wife and three small children. They built a small house, put up a shed for the horses, and one cow, bought a few groceries, and had thirty-seven cents left over.[2]

Elvy didn't waste time looking for any relief agency. He walked about eighty miles down into Colorado, where he found work in the sugar beet country. He had to leave the team so his wife could haul water from a small creek a mile away. When fall came, Elvy returned and plowed the required number of acres and seeded it with winter wheat.[3]

It was much the same with all of us. We had no equipment and did not want to buy any, as we knew we were not going to stay longer than the required period. It was cheaper for us to hire our forty acres plowed and then rent it on shares than it would have been to buy a plow and horses so that Earle could do our plowing himself. Besides that, Earle knew nothing about plowing or seeding. He had a busy summer ahead without it.

---

2   Elvy Gillaspie was born in Iowa on February 15, 1881. He, his wife Jessie, and three children were farming outside of Moravia, Iowa, in 1910. His son Harold was four years old, his son Walter was two years old, and his daughter Wilma had just been born. In 1920, the US Census taker recorded that Elvy and Jessie (who was also born in Iowa) had four sons and two daughters (1910 US Census, 1920 US Census, World War I Draft Registration Cards, 1917–1918, www.ancestry.com, accessed March 3, 2008).

3   The beginning of this paragraph could be a criticism of New Deal programs during the Great Depression, or of government aid more generally. Laura Ingalls Wilder, who opposed the New Deal vehemently, included antigovernment messages in several of her *Little House* books. See Anita Clair Fellman, *Little House, Long Shadow: Laura Ingalls Wilder's Impact on American Culture* (Columbia: University of Missouri, 2008), especially chapters 2 and 3.

We could not expect much of a crop with the late planting. We had already found that the older settlers east of Chugwater sowed their winter wheat or barley in the fall in order to benefit from the fall rains and winter snow.

The Casters had come through the lonely winter very well.

"The boys were a big help to me," Luther said. "They kept the ice out of the stock tank and they chopped wood and helped take care of the stock. We got along pretty good."

Mrs. Caster added, "Osa and I pieced together a quilt from scraps that my mother sent me, and we had plenty of work with all the snow tracked in. Just keeping eight people fed is a job. It was lonesome, though, and I'm sure glad to see all the new people here, especially Dr. Day."

Chugwater, ca. 1913-1916. This is the central part of town. The lettering on the building on the right reads "Sanitary Barber Shop." CLARICE WHITTENBURG COLLECTION, BOX 11A, FOLDER 16, AMERICAN HERITAGE CENTER, UNIVERSITY OF WYOMING

CHAPTER TWELVE

Homesteading

OUR MOST PRESSING NEED WAS FENCING. WE HAD NO WAY TO KEEP OUR stock in or other stock out until our fences were built.[1] Earle put in nearly three miles of fence that summer. First he had to dig the post holes, which was a hard job. The spring rains were over and the ground was dry and hard. Many times he had to use a bar to get the hole started and then dig on down with the post-hole spade. Earle had never done any hard manual labor in his life, but in spite of blistered hands and a lame back, he kept on.

He fenced the forty-acre field first, which we had hired a man to plow and then rented out on shares.[2] That crop had to be protected from any stray stock. Then there was the remaining fence on the half-mile east side and our half-mile next to old Dave Gillaspie. The fence along the half-mile west side was finished at last, and we had the place enclosed. Finally we put a fence around the house and garden.

Early in the spring, a young bachelor had been plowing when a severe electrical storm came up. The man and his team were all killed by lightning. We also heard of many head of stock being killed when they were near a wire fence, so Earle put in two metal stays between each fence post. The stays were twisted wire, which were placed over

---

1   "Barbed wire made . . . the homestead possible on the dry plains" (Webb, *The Great Plains*, 318).

2   Earle allowed someone else to plant and take care of the wheat crop; they shared the produce at harvest. The Smiths were doing the absolute minimum in order to get title to the land, and Earle was not doing the crop work himself.

the top wire and then twisted down, securing the lower wires, and driven into the dirt to make a ground for lightning. This saved on fence posts and made a good fence. All this added to the work of fencing, so the job seemed endless. About the only thing I could do to help was to hold the wire puller taut after Earle had fixed it on the posts while he drove in the staples.

After the fencing was completed, Earle helped Luther and Herschel finish Dr. Day's house. They built a half basement of concrete with a storage room behind, which served as a cool room. There was a large combination kitchen-and-dining room, and above this they built a living room and one bedroom. The construction was built into a slope, so they could use fairly large windows on the south and east. This made the basement light and pleasant. There was good reason to have shelter from the whistling west and north winds, and it was always so dry in Wyoming that there was never any difficulty with damp walls.

I was still having difficulty with my bread. Mrs. Day baked lovely bread, and she tried to help me. She couldn't give me more precise measurements than "just taking some flour and water and your yeast, add a little lard, and mix it up." We had no sort of refrigeration, and we didn't get to Chugwater often enough to get yeast, so we all depended on a starter. I had to set the sponge in the evening with water from the boiled potatoes, flour, and the starter saved from the last bread sponge.

In the morning, I would take out a pint of this sponge and mix it with more flour, salt, and shortening to make a dough. I had to save some of this for the next batch of bread. It was all guesswork, and sometimes my guesses didn't turn out so well. I let the dough rise, kneaded it down, let it rise again, and made it into loaves. Again it had to rise. In the meantime, I attempted to have the oven ready for it to bake. I usually had the oven too hot, or else I started the oven too soon and it

Chugwater, 1916. This photograph shows more of the town's surroundings. The four buildings of the previous photograph are visible just to the left of the center of the frame. It appears that the one farthest to the left has been painted white.
WYOMING STATE ARCHIVES, DEPARTMENT OF STATE PARKS AND NATURAL RESOURCES

was cooled down by the time the bread was ready. Both Mrs. Caster and Mrs. Day chuckled at my troubles.

Mrs. Day and I each baked our bread just once a week, so we agreed to exchange a pint of starter so it would be fresher. I saved starter for her and she did the same for me, but I always suspected that she also saved her own and managed to keep it fresh some way. Her bread was always so much better than mine, hard as I tried.

With the fencing finished, we turned to the next task of moving our house up onto the hill, where we would be close to the other three

Laura, their horse, and the rock stable. This building served as their home while they were building their two-story house. LAURA GIBSON SMITH PAPERS, IOWA WOMEN'S ARCHIVES, UNIVERSITY OF IOWA LIBRARIES

families. Earle gathered cobblestones from a snake-infested draw about a quarter of a mile away, and hauled them up to the spot we had chosen. That was the summer that Earle killed over sixty rattlesnakes of all sizes, from small ones to huge ones with fourteen rattles.

Dr. Day's dog, Fanny, was responsible for finding many of the snakes. She would hear them buzz, and would start circling around them at a safe distance. Usually, rattlers will sound their warning and then, unless crowded, they will slither off out of sight. Fanny kept circling the snakes and kept them rattling until Earle could get there with some weapon and kill them. He broke the handles on hoes, shovels, spades, or anything else handy with his determination to kill them.

It was seldom that he made a trip down into the draw to gather rocks without killing a snake. It was a long, hard pull up out of the draw, so Earle could not bring much of a load of stones at a time. But finally he thought he had enough.

We had to go to Chugwater for cement and lumber to make the forms. That was my first trip to the city. We used Luther's team and wagon. Early in the morning, we started out in the lumber wagon and plodded off across the prairie to the town, nearly twenty miles away. It was the first time I had been over that route since the Andersons had brought us to Buckmaster's shack nearly a year before. A trail had been worn by the men going to Chugwater, so there was no puzzle about where to go.

Several more families had come out that spring and built small houses which we passed along the way; there were others within view. We might all be crazy, but to Earle and me, it meant a great deal that older and more experienced people had taken claims with such faith and optimism.

We could see Andersons' house in the distance, but with the team and wagon we weren't about to drive miles out of our way. So we didn't stop to see them.

We could see Herschel Sell's house and Claude Long's place a few miles to the north. We passed Clarence Duvall's dugout, where he still lived. It was nothing but a hole in the ground. The sides were built up of sod, and there was a roof over it. There was a door and a window on one side. Duvall had lived there for three years.

Eagle Rock, where a pair of eagles nested every year, loomed above us as we drove around the curve down Chugwater Creek and on into town.

Chugwater had one dusty street and a small general store. The owner carried a variety of goods, including staple groceries and work clothes. He had a lumberyard where we bought a minimum of lumber and cement. His prices were outrageous to us, and whenever possible we bought things in Cheyenne and had them shipped to Diamond. The Swan Land and Cattle Company also had a small grocery store in Chugwater, but their prices were just as high. Nothing fresh was handled in either store. There were three or four houses, and that comprised the whole town.[3]

Earle watered and fed the horses, and while they rested we made our purchases and loaded the wagon. Then we were ready to start the long journey home again. It had taken us nearly four hours to get to Chugwater. It took us five hours to return home with the load.

I hadn't thought to take any lunch, so we bought a box of crackers, a couple of cans of Vienna sausages, bread, and cheese, which with a jar of water I had brought made our lunch as we jogged along home. Distant rain and long shadows changed the color of the hills. It was beautiful.

All summer I had wanted to go to Chugwater, but that once was enough. Joggling along for forty miles on a spring seat in a lumber wagon over a rough trail, bumping over stones, down into gullies, and up on the other side, made a long day. I admitted that one trip satisfied me.

———

Day after day Earle worked on building a stable. He built the forms the same size as our basement house, digging out only a little for a foundation. He made spaces for the three windows the same size. This building would have a walk-out door on the same level, instead of a cellar door that went down into the living room like we had at the other house. The building was twelve feet by sixteen feet, and would be used as the stable eventually. We lived in it while we built our larger house.

---

3   The *Wyoming State Business Directory* gave Chugwater's population in 1912 as 50. Two years later it was given as 150. Laura's description matches the former more than the latter. For more on Chugwater's growth and subsequent history, see the afterword (*Wyoming State Business Directory, 1912–1913*, 203; *Wyoming State Business Directory, 1914* [Denver: Gazetteer, 1914], 103).

Earle knew absolutely nothing about laying up cobblestones, but he managed a very good job. He may have been a little stingy on his cement mixture, but the building stood for a good many years. We called in Herschel Sells again. He charged $3.00 a day when he used his team and $1.50 when he worked without them.

The two men unbolted the roof of our basement house, lifted the roof onto the wagon, and hauled it intact up to the cobblestone house. There they bolted it onto the plate, and we were ready to move in. It took only one load on the wagon to bring up the furniture, the windows, and door.

Earle put the windows in with nails temporarily at the sides to hold them. Ordinary barn-door hinges were seated in place on the door, and we were ready to settle down in our new home for a while. Herschel helped to get the stove in place and put the stovepipe up through the roof. While I unpacked the few dishes and utensils, the men made one more trip and brought up the privy—all in one piece. Earle didn't forget the stakes and wire to hold it down.

I was delighted to be up on the hill. Instead of being down in the lowland where I couldn't see anybody or anything, now I could see the neighbors. The Days were just across the road; the Casters were a quarter of a mile to the south; on further south I could see Dave Gillaspie's house. A number of other houses were faintly visible in the distance to the south and west. Across the wide undulating valley were hills twenty miles away lifting to the horizon. Fifty miles south I could see Laramie Range.

A few days after we moved, Earle rode Bill the horse to Diamond to get the mail. He brought back quite a stack of papers, magazines, and letters. Earle sat down on the floor in the doorway with his back against the door to glance through them. It was a cool day, and the sun shown in pleasantly. I was getting dinner. I happened to look out the door, and there was a big rattlesnake wriggling his way directly toward the open door and Earle.

"Look!" I screamed. Earle jumped up and all in the same movement slammed the door. He yanked the nails out of the window on the west side facing the road, scrambled out, and ran around the house and began to throw rocks at the snake. There was a crack below the door and no lock. I was afraid the snake would either crawl in under the door or that Earle would knock the door open with the rocks he was raining on the rattler. So I crawled headlong out the window, too.

I stayed a safe distance back while Earle finished off the snake. The door remained firm and the snake was still outside, so I felt pretty silly to think of my dive through the window. Dr. Day and his wife happened to be outside and saw us going headfirst out the window. They couldn't imagine what was going on. They rushed over to find out, but by then the snake was dead.

— • —

The summer was going fast. After the usual formalities of petitions, the county furnished materials for a school building—but the men in the district had to build it. Everyone turned out for that job. The small one-room schoolhouse was located on the southeast corner of the Casters' claim, which was the most nearly central location for all the children. The county arranged for a teacher, Virginia Thompson, to come out and teach, so the children's long vacation would soon be over. The parents were much pleased, and I think the children were, too.[4]

We planned a picnic for the Fourth of July down near Chugwater Creek under the box elder trees. We sent invitations by the grapevine far and wide, and we had quite a crowd. It was the first get-together of any kind. No speeches were made, but there was a lot of friendly visiting. Each of us women took the very best food we had or could get hold of. It was unseasonably cold. The day was chilly and a bit cloudy,

---

4 . The one-room schoolhouse epitomized rural education in the Midwest, and it was replicated in many places on the Great Plains, including Wyoming. See Wayne E. Fuller, *The Old Country School: The Story of Rural Education in the Middle West* (University of Chicago, 1982).

but we were having a good time visiting and eating—until suddenly it began to snow! That stopped the fun. We loaded up in our wagons, buggies, and on horseback and left for the long, cold ride home.[5]

It was a tremendously important day for us when the men came to drill our well. After more than a year of hauling or carrying water, we would finally have all we wanted just a short distance from our door. Since we were up on the highest point, we had to go deeper than either the Casters or Dr. Day had. Our well was 152 feet deep. It cost us a dollar per foot, but we felt that it was worth it. The water was wonderfully cold and good.

While we were drilling our well, when we were down over one hundred feet, the bit broke and they had to pull it out and start an entirely new hole. The bit had broken in two, and that left part of it in the hole where he couldn't drill through the bit.

When one of our neighbors was drilling a well, some practical joker put a bucket of coal down the shaft when nobody was looking. When the drilling continued and that coal came up, they all kidded him that he'd "struck coal."

We ordered a windmill and lumber to put up the tower. When that was up and pumping, we felt we had passed a real milestone. At last I could have all the water I needed or wanted just by holding a pail under the spout. Earle was thankful to be through with the time-consuming task of hauling water.[6]

---

5 Bill Nye, a Wyoming humorist, once joked: "in the summer the snow clouds rise above us and thus the surprised and indignant agriculturist is caught in the middle of a July day with a terrific fall of snow" (Samuel Western, *Pushed Off the Mountain, Sold Down the River: Wyoming's Search for Its Soul* [Moose, WY: Homestead, 2002], 30). However, weather records for Chugwater give high temperatures in the 80s and 90s the week of July 4, 1914. The temperature did fall to 32 on July 6, 1915 (NOAA / National Weather Service preliminary data; Barbara Mayes Boustead, NOAA, e-mail message to author, September 23, 2010).

6 In the arid West, wells might be "anywhere from thirty to three hundred feet deep," and windmills took advantage of a plentiful resource to draw water. They were ubiquitous on farms on the Great Plains. See Webb, *The Great Plains*, 333–348 and Richard L. Hills, *Power from Wind: A History of Windmill Technology* (Cambridge University, 1996), 236–256.

The Robinson School had been built about eight miles away on the road to Chugwater, and Earle obtained the contract to teach there that fall. Our bank account was steadily going down, and even the $50 a month salary that he would get for teaching would be a big help and would produce secure living.

After the Caster School was built, Earle started in earnest to build our permanent home. With nothing but a spade and shovel, he dug out a space about four feet deep so that we would have shelter from the wind and snow to the north and west, but which would still leave space for fairly large windows above ground on the south and east. Thus, in the summer of 1914, we had a "split-level" house.

This time we ordered materials from Cheyenne to be delivered to Diamond, which was much cheaper than buying in Chugwater. That way we only had to haul them five miles instead of twenty. Earle hauled more heaps of smaller rocks from the draw to use for the walls. Herschel helped him put up the forms, three footboards at a time. They mixed the cement by hand and then dumped in the stones, tamping them down to make a good solid wall.

Soon it was time for school to start, and the house was not nearly finished. Herschel would come over each evening when Earle got home from school. Together they would take off the boards, set them up in the new section, and go through the cement-mixing and stone-tamping procedure until that course was full. Saturdays and Sundays they worked all day.

We had one large room in the basement. Three south windows made it light and pleasant, with one smaller window near the stove to the east. The opposite end was the kitchen, with a corner walled off for a storeroom. The south door was built at grade level. Steps led down to the lower floor, and five steps led to the upper floor. There we had a living room and bedroom. We even had a small front porch with a door on the west leading to it. That was a mistake. Nobody in their

The completed rock house on the ridge. "Altogether it was very attractive and comfortable." LAURA GIBSON SMITH PAPERS, IOWA WOMEN'S ARCHIVES, UNIVERSITY OF IOWA LIBRARIES

right mind would sit out there on that porch when the wind was blowing. The wind whipping under that porch roof should have taken the whole roof off, but Earle and Herschel had bolted it on, and it stayed there for forty years.

We had defied all the accepted rules of building on the prairie. Our house was unprotected by any hills. The ranchers chose sites surrounded by hills, where they would have some protection from the cold winds and blizzards. But our house was comfortable, and we were very proud of it. Inside we put on one-inch furring strips, and then added wallboard on the ceiling and walls. We stained the four-by-four ceiling beams and put the wallboards above them, so that we had a beam ceiling. For the walls, we stained strips of barn bats and used them to cover up the joinings of the wallboard. Altogether it was very attractive and comfortable. A heating stove, bed, and dresser made another dent in our bank account. We were even more thankful that Earle would be getting a salary from teaching soon. Shortly after we were settled in our new house, the schoolteacher, Virginia Thompson, came to board with us. That cash helped a bit, as we were getting worried about finances. Our baby was due in February.

Earle obtained a contract to go to Fort Madison, Iowa, in January. A new grammar school had been built and would be ready after Christmas. Earle was elected principal—with a much higher salary than he could get in the Wyoming county school. I began to think that I would do nothing but pack and unpack for the rest of my life.

CHAPTER THIRTEEN

The Funeral

EARLY IN THE SPRING,[1] WE HAD BOUGHT A FOURTH-HAND TOP BUGGY for $7.50. Then we had to have a single harness. Earle already had a saddle. There is something extremely incongruous about a top buggy out on the rough trails of the prairie. This ancient vehicle had a bedraggled top, and the seat was partly worn through, but the springs were fairly good and the wheels and box were solid, so we were satisfied with it.[2]

One Saturday morning, Luther came hurrying up the road. Usually he sent one of the boys on any errands, so we wondered what it was that had brought him to our house.

"The Blacks' little baby died last night, Earle," he said.[3] "They want Dave Gillaspie to make a casket, but he doesn't have any lumber. I haven't got any either; do you have any small pieces we could use?"

---

1   Since the previous chapter essentially finished with an account of the year 1914, it seems that this chapter would begin with Laura's description of 1915. In fact, however, chapters 13 through 16 continue to address events from 1914. Chapter 17 begins Laura's account of the spring of 1915.

2   In 1897, the Sears catalog advertised two top buggy models for $28.95 and $39.90. Using the Consumer Price Index, in 2011, these prices would be $810 and $1,120 (*1897 Sears Roebuck & Co. Catalogue*, New York: Skyhorse, 2007, 644–648. The $7.50 the Smiths paid in 1914 would be about $169 in 2011. Williamson, *MeasuringWorth*, accessed June 29, 2012).

3   Walter Black and his wife Jessie Forbes Black lived about three or four miles from the Smiths. He was born in Missouri in 1881, she in Kansas in 1889, and they had met in Oklahoma. They were married early in January 1914 and this was their first child (Sam Forbes, *Chugwater: Forbes Family Homesteads, Laramie County Wyoming* [Arvada, CO: Privately published, 2008], 2, 8, 16).

Nancy Black gravestone. This stone was placed on the grave in the Little Bear Cemetery in 2008. It replaced a wooden marker that probably dated from 1914. This photograph was taken in 2012. AUTHOR'S COLLECTION

"I think I do, but I'll look and see what I've got." Earle found enough pieces. "Do you want me to help make it?" Earle offered.

"I wish you would," Luther said gratefully. "Old Dave doesn't do much of a job anymore; his eyes aren't good enough."

They went down the hill together to Dave's place, where they carefully made the small casket. Luther guessed at the size they would need for a baby a few days old.

"I'll take it up to our house and see if Laura has anything to fix it up with," Earle said.

He brought the small casket back to our house, and then went over to tell Mrs. Day about it and get her help. She brought some white muslin. I happened to have some cotton batting, so we cushioned the small box with batting and covered it with muslin. I cut up a sheet to tack on the outside. Then we brought the muslin lining up and sewed it onto the outside cloth to make a smooth finish. For a cover, we tacked on more of the sheet, and then padded the top with muslin. It looked very nice. I had never seen either Mr. or Mrs. Black, but I hoped the little white casket would be some comfort to them.

"Ethel Caster said to tell you that you can't go to the funeral, Laura," Earle informed me.

"Why, of course I'm going!" I said. "I don't know the Blacks, but that doesn't make any difference here when there are so few neighbors." He looked embarrassed.

"She said any woman in your condition shouldn't go to a funeral," he insisted. "She's had eight children, so she ought to know." I stayed home.[4]

We wrapped papers around the little casket to keep it clean, and Earle and Dave took it over to the Blacks' early enough for the services that afternoon.

When Earle came back from the funeral, he was very much upset.

"Luther and I got over to the Blacks' home," he said. "Mr. Black came to the door and took the little casket inside. There were a dozen or so men standing around the yard. In a few minutes, Black came to the

---

4 The superstition that a pregnant woman should not attend a funeral is widespread and of long standing; one authority cites a publication that mentioned it in 1672 ("Pregnancy, influences during," in *A Dictionary of Superstitions,* edited by Iona Opie and Moira Tatem, Oxford University, 1996, Oxford Reference Online, www.oxfordreference.com/views/ENTRY .html?subview=Main&entry=t72.e1148, accessed May 15, 2012).

door and beckoned to me. I went over and without any warning he said, 'Professor, would you just say a few words? We couldn't get no preacher.'

"I was so surprised that I couldn't speak, but I nodded. I stood in the doorway. You know what a tiny one-room house they have, and it was full of women. They had put the casket on a couple of chairs."

"What did you say?" I asked.

"I couldn't think of a thing but those verses about 'Suffer the little children to come unto me,' and I recited the Twenty-Third Psalm." He paused. "We all said the Lord's Prayer. If I'd had any idea they'd ask me such a thing, I could have been prepared.

"Then Black said, 'Professor, would you take the casket in your buggy? Everybody else has come in wagons or on horseback.' So we carried the casket out to the buggy and put it on the seat beside me. Black pointed to the corner of their claim where Luther and some of the other men had already dug a small grave. I waited until everyone had gotten into their wagons, and then led the way across the claim to the lonely grave site."

Earle was really not a very pious soul. I waited for him to go on.

"I did manage to think of a short prayer on the way over there," he said. "But I don't have any idea now what I said. Luther and I put the casket into the grave as carefully as we could. Somebody had found some wildflowers and put them on top of the casket. Black took his wife home, and Luther told me that Black is going to put a fence around the grave site tomorrow. I wanted to pick up Dave and get on home, but Luther insisted I come back to the house. All of the women had brought vittles, and Luther said they wouldn't like it if we didn't stop and eat something. 'But they don't have room for so many,' I demurred.

"'You can't disappoint Dave,' Luther said. 'You'll have to come for a little while.' So we rode down to the house and, sure enough, the neighbor women were serving everybody. The men stayed outside. I

View looking east from Nancy Black grave, Little Bear Cemetery. This photograph was taken in 2012. AUTHOR'S COLLECTION

had a cup of coffee and finally came home. Dave said he'd ride home with Luther. It was all the more pathetic because they tried so hard to make the services like we used to have back home."

I thought of that lonely bare hillside grave with the moaning wind blowing over the prairie. . . .[5]

5   Sam Forbes combed through family records to discover that the infant was a girl and she was named Nancy. She is buried in the Little Bear Cemetery in the corner of section 31 of Township R67W T19N. In 2008, a wooden cross marker in the cemetery that read INFANT BLACK was replaced with a stone that reads NANCY BLACK, INFANT CHILD OF WALTER AND JESSIE BLACK, AUTUMN 1914 (Forbes, *Chugwater: Forbes Family Homesteads,* 15–16; Sam Forbes, e-mail message to author, June 25, 2012).

Chapter Fourteen

Home Life

Our husbands always thought that Jessie Day and I had too many ideas—especially the day that we decided we needed some beauty around our houses. There was nothing but gravel and grass near the houses, and we wanted some flowers.

We decided on an expedition up through a swale on their place where we might find some wildflowers to transplant. We were well armed. Each of us took a pail and a long-handled spade. Jessie persuaded Dr. Day to load his revolver and show us how to use it. Each of us carried a long stick to swish through the grass and scare the rattlesnakes away.

The men refused to go with us on such a foolish errand and merely laughed at us. They did order us not to bring back any cactus if we should find any.

We started up the hollow through the deep grass, swishing our sticks with every step. We were scared, but nobody had seen a rattler up through there. Rattlesnakes were usually out on the sunny, bare hillsides. We began to feel a little more confident. We started talking about different flowers we had seen during the summer, and wondering if we would recognize them since the blossoms were gone.

Suddenly we heard a *buzzzzz.*

We stood absolutely still for a second, and then we dropped everything we had, turned, and tore down the trail for home as fast as we could go. We picked up our skirts and ran until we were breathless.

"I don't dare leave that revolver back there," Jessie gasped.

"Well, we'll just have to go back and get everything," I agreed. "I hope we can find the gun in that high grass."

We could see the pails, but they looked miles away. Going along step by hesitant step, watching ahead of us on both sides, we slowly retraced our way up the little valley. Finally, we were within a few feet of the pails. With our eyes and ears alert, we retrieved our possessions. Luckily, we found the revolver—as well as our other weapons. The rattler had escaped, as rattlers usually will, after giving his gentlemanly warning.

Swishing the grass again on our trip back to the house, we agreed that we didn't particularly care for wildflowers anyway.

The men teased us about coming back so soon. "Couldn't you find any flowers?" the doctor asked.

"We walked quite a ways up there, and we didn't see any. So we decided to put it off," Mrs. Day replied. It was a long time before we confessed what had actually happened.

———

Bill was a shrewd horse. If Earle didn't want to use him, he would let Earle walk up to him anytime out in the pasture. But Bill seemed to have an uncanny ability of knowing when he was about to be put to work. Then he would let Earle come within a few feet of him, and then snort and race for the other end of the pasture a mile away. Earle frequently had to walk miles before he could catch the horse.

That situation demanded a smaller pasture and more fencing. We built a fence north and south, which divided the half-section midway. We also built a small pen around the stable. That gave Bill only half as much area to play games in as he had previously.

Whenever Earle had Bill saddled, he had to make a flying leap onto his back, and Bill would be off and away as soon as one foot was in the stirrup. But when I—or any other woman—got on Bill, he was like an old plow horse and could scarcely be urged off a walk.

The school term opened and Earle began driving the eight miles every day over to the Robinson School to teach. The top fell off the buggy and the whole vehicle gradually became more and more rattly. Herschel Sells helped us work on the house, and at last we had it finished and moved in. Even then we didn't have the pleasure of sleeping in the bedroom. There was no other place in the area for our teacher to board, so we took her in and gave her the bedroom while we slept on the sanitary cot downstairs.

It was wonderful to have more room. We uncrated our mission furniture, which was comprised of a table, two rocking chairs, and a straight chair. Instead of hard wooden kitchen chairs, we now had real chairs with springs in the seats and simulated leather upholstering to sit on! I think now that the black mission furniture was some of the ugliest ever manufactured, but we were very proud of it then.

We made a small bookcase out of boxes that we had packed books in, and we spread our few volumes on the shelves. These included a set of *Britannica* encyclopedias. A heating stove was necessary for upstairs, so we had ordered it from a catalogue, as well as a bed and dresser.

Downstairs, I still had only the cupboards made of packing boxes with a curtain around it. A drop-leaf table, which Earle had made from boards, was my work table, dining table, sewing table, and anything else we needed a table for. Even my kitchen range calmed down and lost some of its malignancy. We had a real concrete chimney, so instead of the stovepipe going straight up through the roof, it went over from the stove to the chimney. That alone calmed down the draft to some extent, so there wasn't a roar constantly as all that heat tried to go straight up the stovepipe.

Mrs. Day showed me more about the dampers and how to regulate the stove. There was a damper in the pipe to be opened when I started the fire. But if I closed it too much, the lids would pop off the stove and shower soot all over the place. Another damper routed the heat around the oven. Mrs. Day showed me that I could lift one of the back lids off and slow down the blaze that way. Gradually I conquered the stove, but I was likely at any time to forget to put in more wood or coal. I baked beans and made rice pudding.

I was always busy. Our diet was not as limited as when we'd had to depend on food from Chugwater, but we still could get no fresh meat or fresh vegetables. We sent to a mail-order house in Kansas City for staples. Ten-pound boxes of dried peaches, apricots, and raisins helped out on the fruit. Canned vegetables, hams, and bacon were much cheaper—even when we paid the freight from Kansas City to Diamond. It was simpler to haul from Diamond, since it was only five miles, instead of the twenty from Chugwater. One or another of the neighbors went to Diamond every week for the mail, and would bring back supplies for everyone in the neighborhood.

Washing on the board was now my toughest proposition, but at least I had plenty of water. I kept the reservoir in the stove full of water, and any extra water I needed I had to heat on top of the stove in the boiler. I had been taught to boil all the white clothes, and I stuck to that idea even though, as the weather became colder, the windows all over the house steamed up until I couldn't see out.

The air was so dry and the wind so strong that I could go back and take down the clothes at the first end of the line by the time I had hung the line full. Talk about automatic dryers! Sheets snapped and tore, bath towels raveled, and all the starch was whipped out of my dresses until I gave up trying to starch them. Shirts flung their sleeves wide, and work pants straightened out like a pair of wind socks. I nearly always had to chase some clothing down the pasture; the clothespins couldn't hold them on the line.

The simple life doesn't always mean simplified housekeeping. I had a broom and a dustpan. The fine sand blew in around the windows, and we tracked sand and gravel and mud in at the door. There was always cleaning to do.

My mother sent me a layette for the coming baby, but I still had sewing to do. The south window in the basement was a delightful place to sew. The sun shone in warmly, the wind didn't scream so loudly in the basement, and I could see far across the brown prairie. I could see Casters' house, the roof of Dave's house, and the schoolhouse. In the afternoons, with the sun at the right angle, I could see houses ten miles away. Over the top of that hill I could see anyone coming on the old trail to Chugwater. Earle still drove Bill and the ancient buggy over that trail to school every day.

One evening I happened to be at the north window when I happened to see a strange apparition coming down the trail. It trotted down the long, gentle hill at a fast pace and stopped at our gate. I could not make out what it was, besides a horse. Finally, as he drove into our yard, I saw that it was Earle! The buggy had given up; the reach was broken just in back of the front axle. Earle was left in the seat, which was still fastened to the buggy box and rear wheels, while Bill was still hitched to the front wheels. Earle pulled into our yard and hauled the rear wheels out of the buggy box. He then stood on the front axle, braced his hands on Bill's flanks, and trotted home like a Roman charioteer. A few days later we hauled the wrecked buggy home, patched it up, and went on using it.

Chapter Fifteen

The Diamond Ranch

WE RECEIVED AN INVITATION FROM MR. RAINSFORD TO LUNCH WITH him on a certain day. It was like a command from the president. For a young couple like us, despised homesteaders, to be invited to the home of an important rancher was a tremendous compliment.[1]

The only homesteaders who had been on the Diamond Ranch were a few men who had gone fishing in his trout stream. They were not accustomed to private streams, and so they were amazed and angry when a couple of Rainsford's cowboys drove the homesteaders' horses into Rainsford's corral and locked the gate. The homesteaders were twenty miles from home, and were truly puzzled about his inhospitality. After a couple of hours of haggling, they were finally allowed to take their horses and leave. But they received a stern warning not to fish on his ranch again.[2]

---

1   George Rainsford was born before the Civil War to a wealthy family in New York. He moved to Wyoming in the late 1870s and developed an enormous ranch of over 7,000 acres. By 1900 there were around 2,800 horses on the ranch. However, between 1905 and 1907 the federal government brought suit against him for illegal fencing of the public domain. He was forced to buy a significant amount of land and pay several large fines. By 1910, he had reduced his stock to the hundreds, but he still lived a genteel life by Western standards (*History of the Diamond Ranch* [New York: Privately published, 1919], 2–3, Subject file: Ranch—Diamond, Ghugwater, Wyoming, Rs151, American Heritage Center, University of Wyoming, Laramie, Wyoming).

2   A 1981 newspaper article noted that "he had no use at all for the homesteaders and other residents of the area" ("The Diamond Ranch," *Star Valley Independent*, Afton, Wyoming, May 21, 1981, Subject file: Rainsford, George Dean, B-R136-gd, American Heritage Center, University of Wyoming, Laramire, Wyoming).

Stable at the Diamond Ranch, ca. 1910s. "He took us to the big stables and admonished us not to call them barns." DIAMOND RANCH PHOTOGRAPH FILE, AMERICAN HERITAGE CENTER, UNIVERSITY OF WYOMING

Earle hitched Bill up to the old buggy and said, "I wish you could ride a horse. Rainsford once told somebody, 'You know this used to be country for horses and cattle; now all they can raise is top buggies and babies.'"

We took the trail to Diamond that led up to the inevitable gate leading to Mr. Rainsford's ranch. It was more than ten miles from this front gate up to his house over a rough trail. We wound through low hills and small valleys, and crossed a bridge over a clear brook. Mr. Rainsford had built his English-style stone ranch house in a valley where there was a cool, gurgling stream. Cottonwoods and box elders made it a beautiful green spot. Pines covered the hillside behind the buildings.

Mr. Rainsford was an architect from New York who came to Cheyenne and liked the West. A number of business buildings still stand in Cheyenne which he designed.[3] We were both anxious to make a good impression on him, because he was a real figure in our eyes. Fortunately, we had arrived at the house at the proper interval before lunch. It wasn't too easy to drive more than fifteen miles and not arrive too early or too late. Mr. Rainsford met us at the door. He was a tall, slender man with sharp eyes. He looked just like my ideal of a Kentucky colonel. He even wore a goatee.

I was shown to the powder room. There was actually running water in the house, carried down from a tank on the hillside above. It was the first washbowl and flush toilet I had seen since we'd stayed at the hotel in Cheyenne several months before. The house was beautifully furnished, and I thought it was a very desirable place to live. Mr. Rainsford put us at ease at once. I had very little social contact with people other than my own age group, and I was rather shy. But Mr. Rainsford was very tactful, and soon had both of us talking.

The butler announced lunch very shortly, and what a feast that was to us! Actual steak! A tossed salad, and all the other good things, ending with lemon meringue pie! At least both of us had been taught

---

3   Buildings designed by Rainsford still standing in Cheyenne include the Corson House at 209 East 18th Street, the William Sturgis House at 821 East 17th Street, and the Van Tassel Carriage House (now the home of the Cheyenne Artists Guild) at 1701 Morrie Avenue. Cheyenne has registered a residential section of the city bounded by Morrie, 22nd, Warren, and 17th Streets as the "Rainsford Historic District" on the National Register of Historic Places (Cheyenne Artists Guild, "A Brief History about the Cheyenne Artists Guild," http://cheyenneartistsguild.weebly.com/history-of-the-guild.html, accessed May 15, 2012; National Register of Historic Places, "State Listings, Wyoming—Laramie County," http://nationalregisterofhistoricplaces.com/WY/Laramie/state.html, accessed May 15, 2012).

the use of a salad fork, and we enjoyed the meal. I did make one boner. When we had been served the main course, Mr. Rainsford asked, "Mrs. Smith, would you have coffee now or with dessert?"

Overanxious to show my social knowledge, I replied, "I'll have mine with the dessert, please."

He looked at me, hesitated, then said kindly, "I'm afraid you are tired after that long ride. John, bring coffee for all of us now."

"How do you occupy yourself in the winter, Mr. Rainsford?" I asked. "We left last winter, right after that big snow."

As though it was scarcely worth comment, Mr. Rainsford explained, "I spend most of my winters in Egypt. I usually take only a few days to see my people in New York, arrange to ship some horses out here, and then go on to the warmer weather. I have a very good ranch foreman, so there is nothing I can do here until spring." He turned the conversation back to Earle.

"Mrs. Lingwall told me that you had a hard time getting to Diamond in all that snow. You had better get your snowshoes fastened on better next time. Don't you know you could have been buried in the snow in one of those gullies? The coyotes would have found you before any of the neighbors did!"

"I feel pretty silly about that," Earle admitted. "You see, I put a big nail in my suitcase just to poke the snow and ice out of those holes. Then I couldn't find that nail until I emptied my suitcase in the hotel in Cheyenne. I'd been using my pocketknife at home and left it on the table. I'd never been in the habit of carrying a knife, so I didn't pick it up unconsciously the way I might have if I'd always carried one. Here I had more twine to fix the snowshoes with, but I couldn't, just 'cause of that darn nail!

"I have to admit I was scared. The first time I went down into the deep snow, I hauled myself up with the suitcase. I figured I could keep doing that," Earle continued.

"Let's go outside and look around," Mr. Rainsford said when we had all finished. "I want to show you my horses." He took us to the big stables and admonished us not to call them barns. There were rows of box stalls along the sides. Sleek heads reached out to be patted as we passed. In the tack room were saddles of all types, from small English saddles to big Western ones. The carriage house was a revelation to me. There was a phaeton, a break, a brougham, and a number of carts, including some training carts.

"I raise horses for the carriage trade in the East—polo ponies and park riding horses. We train them here, and use all these vehicles.

"The colts are never broken as they are on most ranches. We handle them and baby them from the very time they are born. There is no 'breaking.' These horses would be ruined if they were allowed to run wild and were then brought in, lassoed, and broken to ride." He was quite vehement in his explanation.

"I noticed that you use a tiny diamond shape for your brand, Mr. Rainsford," I remarked.

"Yes, I'm compelled to have a brand for my own protection," he explained. "But I make it as small as possible. You can see on the left flank of this horse; it hardly shows. Certainly not enough to be a blemish, and I like to think that anyone owning a horse with my diamond brand is proud of it. I never ship a horse out that I'm not proud of."

Sometime later, when Earle was teaching at the school, the father of one of the girls mentioned that he wanted to get a horse for his daughter. Earle told him that if he went out to the Rainsford ranch he could probably get one.

Dr. Day and Earle were about the only homesteaders that were permitted on the place, unless they had come to work. So Earle wrote a letter of introduction to Mr. Rainsford, explaining the situation.

When the man went out and handed Rainsford the letter, he said, "You're the first son-of-a-b—— ever came out here properly introduced! Of course I'll take care of you!"

He sold him a very gentle little old horse for the girl.[4]

---

4   Rainsford sold the ranch between 1916 and 1918 and moved to New York City. He died the day after Christmas in 1935 while wintering in Daytona Beach, Florida. His obituary was carried in the *New York Times* and read: "Announcement was made here last night of the death on Thursday at his winter home in Daytona Beach, Fla., of George Dean Rainsford of the Hotel Plaza, this city, former owner of the Diamond Ranch in Wyoming. He was a bachelor, 79 years old, a son of the late George S. Rainsford, New York Banker. Mr. Rainsford belonged to the City Club of New York and the Denver Club of Denver" (*New York Times*, December 28, 1935, 15).

For a while during the 1950s and 1960s, the Diamond Guest Ranch was operated as a dude ranch. It is now privately owned (Clyde Caster Jr., conversation with author, Laramie County, Wyoming, June 21, 2012).

Chapter Sixteen

Fall and Winter 1914

Prairie dogs are notoriously hard to kill. They scuttle into their burrows at the slightest alarm, and then come out cautiously, barking to their friends if all is clear. If one prairie dog is shot, it usually tumbles into the wide mouth of the burrow, or else it scrambles into the hole for safety, so you never know whether you've hit it or not.

A couple of old friends of ours, Mr. Danforth and Mr. Clove, came out from Ames, Iowa, to investigate the chances for getting a claim. Dr. Day and Earle offered to take them around, although there were no claims nearby that hadn't been filed on. They hitched up the team to the lumber wagon, put on two spring seats, and started out.

While the men were out that day, they passed very near a prairie dog town. A number of animals were sitting outside their holes, chattering as usual.

"I hear the prairie dogs are hard to shoot," Danforth remarked. Without a word Dr. Day pulled his revolver out of his pocket, aimed at the nearest prairie dog, and fired. It tumbled into the hole. Dr. Day put the gun away in his pocket while Danforth stared at him in amazement. Dr. Day didn't say anything. He knew it was an accident.

"Say, you are a good shot, Dr. Day," Danforth gasped.

⸺

Fall came. The grass had been dry for a long time, cured into nourishing feed for the livestock. All the cattle and horses, fed only on the pastures, were plump and sleek. We decided to have the hay cut in some of the low places where it had grown tall, so that we could have feed for Bill without turning him out at night. That would save time and effort on the cold mornings. Earle had been having hay shipped out from town for emergencies.

Herschel Sells came down to do the mowing one Saturday morning, and got quite an area cut. He came in for dinner at noon. I knew that such a big man would have a good appetite, so I worked hard to have a good meal, and plenty of it. He did justice to it.

Then, as he pulled a smelly pipe out of his pocket, he remarked, "I'll go outside to smoke. Always like to smoke after a meal. It gets the taste of the food out of my mouth."

Earle grinned at me; he knew I was furious. The two men went outside where Herschel lighted his pipe. They walked around the house, talking about the best places to mow, and sat down in the sun on the south side of the house. Presently, Virginia the schoolteacher came downstairs. Very matter-of-factly, she asked, "What is the fire out there north of the house?"

"Fire?" I exclaimed and tore upstairs and out of the house to where the men were sitting. "Virginia says there's a fire! Where is it?"

They jumped to their feet, ran around the house, and gaped at our own private prairie fire roaring down across the pasture with the wind driving it faster every second. Earle and Herschel both grabbed gunnysacks, soaked them in the stock tank, and began slapping them futilely at the edges of the fire. In just those few moments the fire had reached the edge of our land a half-mile away.

Dr. Day and his wife came running over. All of the Caster family came on the run, as did Dave Gillaspie. Shortly afterwards, Elvy drove up with his team on the gallop. Everybody who was within sight of the smoke came as fast as they could, but there was nothing anyone could do. The freakish wind blew the fire across the short, brown, dry grass. The fire raced across the corner of McDonald's pasture and reached a plowed field, where it died out. The men piled into Elvy's wagon to make sure it was all burned out.

We women went into the house to rest and talk it over. We were very much subdued. The fire could have burnt some of our houses or injured livestock if it hadn't been stopped by that plowed field.

Herschel felt terrible about it. He thought he must have tossed his match into the dry grass after he'd lighted his pipe. The strong wind did the rest. Earle tried to make Herschel feel better by pointing out that the fire might have been caused by a spark from the chimney.

There was nothing to be done about it, and I think the grass came up thicker the following spring where it had been burned over. I also hoped it had roasted a few rattlesnakes.

The men picked out another good spot farther east on the claim and Herschel went back to work mowing the grass. Everybody else went home while I began washing dishes. I could forgive Herschel for starting the fire, but I could never forgive him for telling me that he smoked his pipe to get the taste of my food out of his mouth!

The days moved on into October, and we all agreed that we didn't want to be caught unprepared for another deep snow this winter. The men went up to the mountains for wood, and all of us had great piles of pitch pine ready to be chopped up. We ordered a sizable list of staple groceries from the mail-order house in Kansas City.

A group around Chugwater had formed a cooperative organization in 1912, and had brought in carloads of various things from time to time. We heard that they now had a carload of flour and a carload of potatoes brought up from Colorado on the siding in Chugwater. The men decided they would stock up on those two items, since the cooperative always sold cheaper than the store could.

"How many sacks of potatoes do you think we should have?" Earle asked.

I had only a vague idea about the size of a sack of potatoes, so I said, "Oh, eight or ten ought to be enough. They should keep all winter."

Earle came home with ten sacks of potatoes purchased at fifty cents a sack. I looked at the tag on the first bag he brought in.

"Earle, these sacks have *one hundred pounds* of potatoes in each one! We've got one thousand pounds of potatoes! A half a ton!" We simply howled. A half-ton of potatoes for three people!

"I think some of the neighbors would be glad to take part of them," Earle said. "I had no idea that many pounds of potatoes were in a bag."

"Why didn't you read the tag?" I asked.

"Well, you said ten sacks! So I bought ten," Earl replied.

Sure enough, some of the neighbors were glad to buy some of our half-ton of potatoes, which saved them from having to haul them out from Chugwater. Even so, we had potatoes three times a day, in every way imaginable that fall, and still we had bags of potatoes crowding the storeroom.

Autumn passed quickly. Cold weather came and the wind blew savagely. The coyotes howled at night, but Earle was home and Virginia Thompson was good company. We had no time to be lonely. Our house was cozy and we were content.

Uncle Billy Robinson opened a small store over near the schoolhouse, where he kept a few staple groceries. Occasionally he would butcher a pig, and Earle would bring home fresh meat. That was a big treat. We could even get eggs from some of the pupils' parents, so cooking was not such a trial. I had been lost without eggs. No cookies, cakes, or puddings. It seemed to me that everything I liked best called for eggs.

I do have to give that kitchen range some credit. I could put a pot of beans flavored with some of Dave's sorghum 'lasses and a ham bone in the oven and let them bake all day, unworried about the electric or gas bill involved. I've never had such baked beans since.

Mrs. Day showed me how to make a most delicious rice pudding. It took four tablespoons of rice, two beaten eggs, some sugar, nutmeg, salt, and two quarts of milk. It was baked slowly for hours. It came out the creamiest, most delectable pudding imaginable. I had to have the fire going anyway for heat, so I always kept good things simmering on the stove that I've never been able to equal since.

Until it became bitterly cold, we couldn't waste fuel by keeping a fire in the heating stove upstairs all day. I usually lighted that fire late in the afternoon so it would be warm by the time Virginia came home from teaching school. I spent my time downstairs by the kitchen range and kept very comfortable.

Christmas of 1914 was a beautiful day. The sun was brilliant, and for a welcome change there wasn't much wind. A few days after Christmas, we packed our clothes and left for Iowa, where Earle would teach grammar school at Fort Madison and I would be close to the hospital where my baby was to be delivered. Our son arrived on February 15, 1915. We named him Bertel.

Chapter Seventeen

Visitors

I HAD TO RETURN TO THE CLAIM BEFORE EARLE'S SCHOOL WAS OUT IN the spring,[1] since we were only allowed five months off during the year. I was delighted when Earle's sister, Laura, offered to go with me and stay until he could come out. She was a registered nurse, so I was vastly relieved to have skilled assistance with my small baby. We always had a lot of fun together, and it was lucky for me she came because I never knew anything about babies. It was a bit overwhelming to me.[2]

Laura expected to see dashing cowboys every day, to go to dances on Saturday night, and all of the rest of the experiences girls in romantic Western novels seemed to have. She was sadly disappointed. There wasn't a cowboy in sight all the time she was with us.[3]

It was still cold when we reached home. It really was home to me by that time. The wide prairies were beautiful and green, even though there was snow in some of the sheltered spots. The high altitude and

---

1   As mentioned in the footnote at the beginning of chapter 13, this chapter begins Laura's description of the events of 1915.

2   Laura Smith, Earle's sister, was about four years older than Earle (1910 US Census, www .ancestry.com, accessed March 6, 2008).

3   By the 1910s, Buffalo Bill Cody's Wild West Show, Owen Wister's novel *The Virginian*, and the development of tourist institutions such as dude ranches and Cheyenne's Frontier Days gave a view of Wyoming's history and economy (and that of the broader West) as built on cowboys and ranching. See Brown, *Wyoming: A Geography*, 68–69, 148–149; Liza Nichols, *Becoming Western: Stories of Culture and Identity in the Cowboy State* (Lincoln: University of Nebraska, 2006); and White, *"It's Your Misfortune and None of My Own,"* chapter 21.

sharp, clear air were exhilarating to me after my months in an Iowa town where they burned soft coal and the air was always full of soot and smoke.

The winter had been fairly mild, so no one had needed the wood and coal we'd left in the bin outside our house. It was there ready for me when I got home. Laura enjoyed her stay with me, but left shortly after Earle came home. I think she was ready to go.

The prairie was always so beautiful in the spring. Larkspur made purple splotches in the low spots, tiny white grass flowers dotted the hillsides, and the detested ball cactus showed its fragile pink blossoms. Later in the summer, the spines of the ball cactus would dry until they were as hard as needles—and just as sharp. They wouldn't penetrate the sole of your shoe, but if you happened to step against the side of one, the spines would go through the leather.

My mother stopped over for a two-week visit with us on her way east. Earle met her at the train in Diamond and brought her home in the usual way, up through the sandy draw. There was no road; only a trail which twisted around between rocks, crossing and re-crossing the winding stream bed. Sometimes it even followed the stream bed for a time. Pungent sagebrush grew up on each side of the steep hillsides. Gradually the trail rose, until the long last hill up onto the plateau where Mother had her first glimpse of the wide prairies, and caught the full force of the wind.[4]

Earle's sister Laura had been terrified of that trail, and I never did enjoy it. I once had to jump out of the wagon when the wheel struck a rock and I thought we were going to tip over. Afterward, I tried to claim that I'd fallen out of the wagon, but I couldn't make that story stick. People do not usually land on their feet when they fall off a wagon.

---

4   Laura's mother, Josephine, was born in November of 1846, and thus was sixty-eight years old in 1915.

Earle, Laura, and Bertel at the homestead. It appears that this may be the top
buggy, but without the top up. LAURA GIBSON SMITH PAPERS, IOWA WOMEN'S ARCHIVES,
UNIVERSITY OF IOWA LIBRARIES

But Mother was not bothered in the least. She was like that; I never
knew her to be afraid of anything. She remarked, "I wouldn't like to be
caught down in that old stream bed just after a big thunderstorm. From
the way it is cut down, the water must really come down in a torrent."

Mother was never a demonstrative or effusive person. She gave
me a perfunctory peck on the cheek, admired the baby, and started to
tell me about a rancher she had talked to on the train. This man had
told her all about the ranchers' problems and what they thought of the

homesteaders. She didn't give us any "Oh, my poor darling, how can you stand the wind and no trees or flowers anywhere?" Instead, she looked around and remarked, "My, you have a marvelous view in every direction. In this clean air you can really see for miles."

Nor did she say "What a tiny house! Don't you get tired going up and down stairs all the time?" What she remarked was, "You have a nice cozy place here. That half-basement is a good idea. It keeps out the wind and makes it easier to heat. When you have to haul all your fuel, that is a big advantage."

She did not sympathize because I had to carry water when Earle was not at home. In complete understanding, she congratulated us that we had our own well and windmill. "You're lucky to have water so close to the house. Earle, you really must have been glad when you got this well and didn't have to haul water anymore. This is wonderful cold water. It tastes far better than ours in California, which has to be brought miles from the mountains."

Mother had lived on a farm most of her life, and was both experienced and open-minded. Earle hitched Bill up and took her all over our place, and we also visited Dr. Day and the Casters. She liked the long views; fifty miles to the far ranges west, and twenty miles to the hills south. "I think these men with the ideas of farming this land are much too optimistic," she said firmly after their tour of inspection. "This was intended for stock country, and that is what it will be in spite of anything you can do. Fourteen inches of annual rainfall won't grow corn, or anything much, except winter grain and hay. I can see it's wonderful for stock, but nobody can make a living for his family on 320 acres. You ought to have four or five sections at least to run enough cattle to make anything."

We agreed. "Those men on Chugwater Flats have plowed up nearly all of their land and put it in wheat. So far, they've had plenty of rain to make good crops. But I'm told that a severe hailstorm can wipe out the whole harvest in half an hour," Earle told her.

"That rancher on the train told me they allow ten to fifteen acres of pasture for each head of stock," Mother said. "Then they put up hay from their irrigated meadows for bad weather in the winter." She admired the wheat on all our claims. It was growing tall and sturdy and heading out well.[5]

"Of course," she said, "it doesn't look like Iowa grain. But nobody could expect to grow it like that on this soil. This looks like a good crop now. Are you going to plow up any more, Earle?"

"No, I'm not," Earle said. "I agree with you that this is primarily grazing land, and since forty acres is all we have to break, we intend to be satisfied with that. Some of the men around here plan to plow up most of their land, but I don't think it's wise."[6]

Mother went on, "My brothers homesteaded in Dakota years ago. They lived in sod houses without half the comfort you have here. They had hail and grasshoppers and drought, but they stuck it out until they could get a patent to the land. While they were there, new regulations were passed that required them to set out so many trees per acre of land to improve the arid conditions. These were called 'tree claims.' My brothers sold their land and moved on to California."[7]

We really didn't need any pep talk, but Mother was a tonic to us and to all the neighbors. She knew what she was talking about, and the

---

5   T. A. Larson stated that "Usually about forty acres of land per cow is needed for a Wyoming ranch . . . Five-thousand-acre units may be satisfactory; 160 acre units are hopeless" (Larson, *History of Wyoming*, 173). The current owners of the Smiths' land suggested that one needs at least twenty acres of good grassland per cow if one doesn't want to have to buy hay (Clyde Caster Jr. and Frances Caster, conversation with author, Laramie County, Wyoming, June 21, 2012).

6   Today Earle and Laura's homestead is part of the Clyde Caster ranch, on which eighty head of cattle run about 2,300 acres (Clyde Caster Jr. and Frances Caster, June 21, 2012).

7   The Timber Culture Act of 1873 enabled homesteaders to file for an additional 160 acres if they planted forty acres of trees; it was reduced to ten acres of trees in 1878. Widespread fraud and the impossibility of growing large numbers of trees on the Plains led to the act's repeal in 1891 (Hibbard, *A History of the Public Land Policies*, 414–423).

men realized it. As for myself, I hated the wind and feared the coyotes and the rattlesnakes, but I could endure all that. As for loneliness, I had no time to be lonely with a small baby to care for.

Mother was greatly amused when I took some rolls out of the oven. Each one was a different size, and each loaf of bread was a different size, too. "You used to make good cake and fudge at home. Your bread is nice and light; you just have to learn about the size to cut off for the rolls," she comforted me.

Chapter Eighteen

Harvests

We were all getting low on wood, so Mr. Caster and his two boys, Dr. Day, and Earle took three wagons and left early one morning for the hills, expecting to be gone two days as usual. About noon the second day, Earle came driving home with Dr. Day's team and only a part of a load of wood. He drove into Dr. Day's yard. Mrs. Day hurried out, knowing that something had happened.

"Dr. Day tripped, fell, and broke his leg," Earle said. "We got him to the station and I came after you so you can go down on the train with him to the hospital in Cheyenne." She hurriedly packed a few things while Earle hitched the horses to the buggy. I went over to see what I could do.

"We'll take care of the chores and everything, Mrs. Day," I said. "Is there anything I can do now?"

"My bread is just about ready to bake," she replied. "You'd better take it home and bake it."

"Don't you worry about a thing," I assured her. "Earle can milk the cow and do other chores. I'll see that the dog is fed, and we'll look after her so she won't get lonesome."

"The chicken feed is in the garage," she said. "I give them about a quart each night, and again each morning. You gather the eggs and keep them; you take the milk, too. Tell Earle to strip the cow good when he milks her. We don't want her to dry up."

There were no hysterics on her part—no questions about how the accident happened. She accepted it as she did every emergency. Earle took her to Diamond, where she found the doctor suffering terribly.

They had improvised a stretcher. When the train came, they had loaded Dr. Day into the baggage car and he was off to the hospital. Even in his misery, he thought of others. "You use my horses anytime you want to, Earle. Just take care of yourselves until I get home."

"We'll look after everything at your place," Earle assured them. "Don't you worry, Mrs. Day. You stay in Cheyenne as long as he needs you."

Fortunately, Luther had some food left for himself and the boys. Earle and the doctor gave him the sandwiches they had left, so he stayed over another day in the hills and came home with his wagons piled high with wood. Cecil and Wayne were proud that they had driven one load home over the rough trail without any mishap.

"Of course they followed me," Luther explained. "And I picked out the best trail I could, so as they wouldn't tip over or anything."

My garden was a terrific disappointment to us. There was one long row of spinach, and that was all that had survived. The previous fall, in our ignorance as well as enthusiasm, we had an area plowed out about the size of a city block. That spring, I had worked for hours hoeing and raking it for a big garden that would supply us with the fresh vegetables we missed so much. I planted everything I could think of: radishes, lettuce, onions, spinach, and cabbage—even potatoes and sweet corn.[1]

We had a few rains in the spring, but not enough to germinate the seeds, so only a few of them even came up. The lettuce appeared and

---

1   Rural women's gardens were important for producing food for the family and for the market. Plots of vegetables and flowers may also have provided women with a psychological outlet; making a garden tamed and domesticated the wild lands in which they lived (Neth, *Preserving the Family Farm*, 19–32 and 59–62; Kolodny, *The Land Before Her*, 35–54).

quickly disappeared—eaten off by the rabbits. We had a few hot rad-ishes. The spinach was the most determined to grow, but neither Earle nor I cared much for spinach. I gathered it and cooked it only when my conscience forced me to. Mother said it was as strong as dandelion greens.

One brilliant moonlit night, I was up with the baby and happened to look out at the garden. Three beautiful deer were in plain sight, cropping the spinach. I opened the door. Even that slight noise star-tled them. They bounded over the fence like it was so much buffalo grass, and were gone in an instant. That was the last of the spinach. I didn't attempt another garden.

We were fortunate enough to find a homesteader who was leaving his claim and had a milk cow with a small calf and another heifer for sale. Most people who had a milk cow preferred to keep her for their own use. Range cows were not good milkers, and they were too wild anyway. Most domestic animals are named, not so much from love and affection, but to identify them. We named our cow "Abbie" because she looked just like a daguerreotype of my great-aunt Abbie.[2] The calf we named "Spot" for the obvious reason that it was spotted. We didn't name the heifer for quite a while, till we learned of her propensity for breaking through any fence in order to go out and search for Gabriel. We named her Evangeline.[3]

It seemed to be the height of luxury to have all the milk, cream, and butter that we wanted. I churned the sour cream in a two-quart fruit

---

2   During the 1830s, Louis Daguerre and several collaborators developed the first commercially viable photographic process. It was announced to the world as the "daguerreotype" and was the most popular way of taking photographs into the 1850s. (Library of Congress, "America's First Look into the Camera: Daguerreotype Portraits and Views, 1839-1864," memory.loc.gov/ammem/daghtml/, accessed August 30, 2012).

3   This is a reference to Henry Wadsworth Longfellow's narrative poem *Evangeline: A Tale of Acadie*, first published in 1847. In it, the heroine, Evangeline, conducts a cross-country search for her lover Gabriel. Longfellow was one of the most popular American poets during the nineteenth century (Maine Historical Society, "Henry Wadsworth Longfellow, Evangeline: A Tale of Acadie," www.hwlongfellow.org/works_evangeline.shtml, accessed May 15, 2012).

jar by shaking it until the small golden specks appeared. Then larger chunks gathered. I had watched my mother make butter hundreds of times when I was a child, so I knew how to work it and wash it. Butter for the table and butter for cooking was something we had never been able to afford before.

A neighbor to the east of us had a scrub bull that had only one idea in his head, and that was to go through, crawl under, or jump over any fence he found. He was a constant nuisance to us, and every few days Earle had to take Bill and chase the bull out of our pasture. Bill was a good cow horse; he would follow, twist, and turn without any guidance, which is remarkable for an Iowa farm horse. One day when Earle was chasing the bull, Bill was doing a good job until the bull suddenly turned. Bill whirled and the saddle girth broke. Earle flew up into the air and came down, still in the saddle, barely missing a big clump of cactus!

A young lad from Fort Madison came out to spend a few weeks with us. He was enthralled with the West, but the one thing he didn't like was the severe electrical storms. Thunderstorms came rolling out of the west with great crashes of thunder and lightning until the air was blue. We stayed indoors until it was over, and then hurried down the hill to see the muddy water pouring down the draw several feet deep where it had been perfectly dry before. In a few hours it would be dry again. The draw drained hills where there was nothing but grass to stop the runoff, so it came fast and furiously for a little while.

Harvest time came. Each of us had a good crop of wheat. A threshing machine was located and hired to come into our neighborhood and thresh all the grain. That first crop was something very special to all of us. It meant needed cash. And, more than that, it meant that we could eventually raise a crop on that land—something we hadn't been at all sure of. It gave everybody a good deal of encouragement.[4]

---

4   For a description of threshing rings and community cooperation, see Neth, *Preserving the Family Farm*, 147–183; for a more poetic description of the process, see Willa Cather, *One of Ours* (New York: Knopf, 1922), 157–159.

For us it meant a little money in the bank to fall back on. For the Casters, Gillaspies, and many of the other families, it meant warm clothing for the children, food for the winter, coal for heating, and above all, it meant encouragement. It rekindled the hope that their move from Iowa to the high prairies would bring prosperity and better living than they could have had on their small farms back home. Hope that they would be able to overcome all the difficulties ahead of them.

That first wheat crop was a tremendous achievement. Farmers sifted golden grains through their fingers, hefted handfuls of it and admired their wheat. All of us were elated with the good heavy wheat that we were able to raise on our own land.

When Elvy Gillaspie had filed on his claim, he had only been able to find 160 acres, which was half of what the government allowed. Nearby, but not adjoining his land, his aunt, an old lady, had filed on another 160 acres. She lived there alone until the summer of 1915, when she was taken sick and passed away. In such cases where the person who filed on the land does not get his patent for any reason, the land reverts to the government and someone else may file on it. Elvy needed that land, and we all felt that he should have first right to file on it since it was in his family. He came hurrying up to our house late one afternoon, terribly excited.

"Earle," he said, "I just heard that Mr. Brain is going to take his oldest boy to Cheyenne tomorrow and file on my aunt's claim. Is there anything we can do about it? It's too late to get to the train today."[5]

---

5   Both a Frank Brain and a Fred Brain appear in an accounts receivable ledger for the Swan Mercantile Store in Chugwater in 1914. Fred Brain was born in England around 1888, and Frank was born in Iowa around 1890, so it is likely that they were brothers. It is unclear which was hoping to file on the homestead. There was also an Allan Brain, who was born in Iowa around 1900, living in the neighborhood in 1920 (1920 and 1930 US Censuses, www.ancestry .com, accessed August 10, 2010; "Accounts Receivable—Swan Mercantile Store, Chugwater, Wyoming, Nov. 30, 1914," Box 29, Folder 8, Swan Company Records, 1877–1984, Collection 11470, American Heritage Center, University of Wyoming, Laramie, Wyoming).

"I don't know what we could do, unless we could get there before they do," Earle replied. "We would have to ride or drive."

"My old horses couldn't go that far," Elvy said. "It's over fifty miles, and I don't think I could ride a horse that far anyway."

"I'll go over and see Mrs. Day," Earle said. Mrs. Day had returned from Cheyenne by that time, but the doctor had not been able to come home yet. Earle told her the situation quickly and, like the rest of us, she wanted Elvy to get the rest of the land.

"If you would let me take Pet," Earle said, "I'll hitch her up with Bill to the buggy and we'll start out as soon as we get the chores done. Pet gets along better with Bill than Snip does, and he's quieter."

"You just take her," Mrs. Day said without the slightest hesitation. "I'm sure that's what the doctor would say if he were home."

Elvy hurried home. Earle gave the horses a good feed of oats and hustled through his chores. I prepared a quick supper for him and wrapped up some sandwiches for both men. Earle hitched up Pet and Bill. Snip was still munching oats and didn't seem to mind that her partner was leaving. The men had always worked the three horses together interchangeably, and since Snip was the finicky one, she had been accustomed to being left alone.

Earle told me about the trip when he returned home. "I picked up Elvy and we started off across the prairie. Neither of us knew anything but the general direction. It would have been a whole lot easier if Elvy could have ridden horseback. We could have gone through places where we couldn't drive the buggy.

"There was no road, not even a trail. There was nothing to guide us except the telegraph line that ran from Cheyenne to Chugwater. We just followed that line. We had to go through ranch land, but we knew where the gates were in the fences. It was mostly open prairie, though. It must have been forty-five or fifty miles, altogether.

"When we got to Cheyenne, we put the horses in the feed barn. As soon as the Land Office opened, we were there. We filed the claim before Mr. Brain got there. He came in just as we got the thing signed up. He was mad as hell. He'd been sure no one could beat him to the Land Office because he'd left by train the day before.

"We stayed all day and the next night to give the horses plenty of rest, and then drove back."[6]

---

6 This account of riding to help Elvy file his claim was actually told by Earle Smith to Alan Andersen in 1983. See also the afterword for more details about Andersen's role in the assembling of *Almost Pioneers* (Alan Andersen, telephone conversation with author, November 21, 2008).

Chapter Nineteen

Alone

THREE MONTHS IS A SHORT SUMMER. IN LATE AUGUST, EARLE HAD TO return to Fort Madison again to teach. The last weeks were busy ones, hauling wood from the mountains, getting coal, and preparing everything for me to spend the next several months alone.

I soon worked out my new routine. I was up early every morning. My small human alarm clock demanded his breakfast by daybreak. There was always washing on the board, ironing and cleaning, baking and cooking. If only we could have dressed babies as sensibly then as we do now. Of course floors were cold in those days, and babies needed warm clothes, but surely not as many as we used to put on them. First a woolen band, then a knit woolen shirt, a diaper, a wool slip, at least one cotton slip, and a white dress made every morning a battle with a squirming baby. Long woolen stockings and shoes completed the outfit. It made much more washing and ironing than the little knit outfits or jeans that the youngsters wear now.

In the afternoons, while the baby took his long nap, I carried in water to fill the reservoir in the range and the teakettle and the extra bucket of water we kept. I carried in enough coal to last overnight, and wood for a quick fire in the morning to get the place warmed fast. The nights were cold.

Before dark I had everything buttoned up and the doors locked. It would have taken a major catastrophe to get me outdoors after dark.

Earle had tried to reassure me about the coyotes. "They're more afraid of you than you are of them," he said.

I retorted, "There is no coyote in this world that could be as scared of me as I am of him."

I never saw the coyotes in the evening, but I could always hear their mournful howling. Each morning, shortly after daylight, I would see them sneaking along the edges of the draw. Sometimes there would be four or five of them padding along steadily, seemingly paying no attention to anything. But any noise would send them sprinting at top speed out of sight in a moment.

Colder weather sent the snakes to their winter quarters underground, so we were rid of that menace for a time. We turned Bill out into Dr. Day's pasture with his old friends Pet and Snip. I had no use for him. One of the Caster boys did the milking for me, and I gave them half of the milk. I was still not a very good pioneer. Our little house was warm and cozy, the wind could whistle and the snow could come. But while I was safe, I was lonesome. Dark seemed to come so early as autumn advanced. I had my housework and sewing in the daytime, but during the evenings there was nothing but a limited supply of reading material and my fancywork. Fancywork always seemed to be a waste of time to me, so I couldn't get much interested in it.

My old problem of baking bread was more difficult with the cold nights. I had to set the bread at night and then keep up a fire in the heater to keep the dough warm. I wasted a good deal of coal. Sometimes I put on coal and covered it with ashes, only to have it flame up. I'd have to let it burn down and then try again before I managed to have it just right to smolder all night and keep the bread warm in the corner behind it.

Occasionally Dr. and Mrs. Day would come over in the evening, but she was teaching at the home school that year, so she was busy and tired by night.[1]

More than ever, I enjoyed the south windows in the basement. I could see the youngsters tumbling out of the schoolhouse door at recess. I could hear their shouting when they played three ol' cat, or other games.[2] Occasionally someone drove past on their way to Diamond or Chugwater. Whoever went to Diamond brought the mail for the entire neighborhood, and whenever the neighbors went to Chugwater they brought out anything I needed. But that was seldom. There was nothing fresh to be had, and we had laid in our supply of staples for the winter.

---

[1] "Home school" here refers to the local schoolhouse built on the Casters' homestead, not what in the twenty-first century is known as "home-schooling." It was the school for their immediate neighborhood. Apparently Jessie Day was the teacher for this term, rather than Virginia Thompson.

[2] "Three ol' cat" was played with a ball and three bases, runners, and fielders. Along with other "ol' cat" games—one ol' cat, two ol' cat, four ol' cat, and tip-cat—it is considered one of the predecessor games to American baseball. See David Block, *Baseball Before We Knew It: A Search for the Roots of the Game* (Lincoln: University of Nebraska Press, 2005), 127–133.

CHAPTER TWENTY

Ladies Aid Club

AGAIN I HAD TO RETURN EARLY TO THE CLAIM.[1] WE WERE DETERMINED that there could be no question about our maintaining residence on the homestead the required time, so I was there more than seven months each year. This time it was easier. I knew what supplies I needed to take with me from Cheyenne. There was wood and coal already in the bin. Luther met me in Diamond with his wagon. We followed the trail up through the draw, and I was back on the claim for my last stint. That fall would complete the three years, and we could get our patent to the land.[2]

We had decided that there was no use for us to try and make a living on 320 acres. Some of the neighbors planned to sell out and leave, so we could have bought more land. But we had no capital to invest in more land or cattle. Nevertheless, it was good to be back. The weather was still cold, but it was a dry cold and was not penetrating. It seemed to me that the wind was slightly more gentle.

I had to give the house a good cleaning, for sand had sifted in during the winter. I did not attempt another garden. Mrs. Day and I had another brainstorm. Both of us had been accustomed to clubs and

---

1   With this chapter Laura begins her account of the events of 1916.

2   Laura and Earle counted their three years homesteading in this way: August 1913 to August 1914, August 1914 to August 1915, and August 1915 to August 1916. They lived on the claim for at least seven months out of each of those one-year periods.

various activities, and we missed them. So we figured the other women did too. We decided to start a club, and not to waste any time about it.[3]

The day after Earle returned at the end of his school year, we gave him a list of all the women we knew of, and sent him off on Bill to invite them to our schoolhouse a few days later for a party to organize a club. We thought we could meet every two weeks in the summertime, when we could take advantage of the warmer weather.

Earle came home just before dark. His face was burned; he was weary and peeved. He limped into the house after unsaddling the horse.

"Are the women all coming?" I asked eagerly.

"I don't know and I don't care," he growled. "Do you realize that I have ridden over twenty miles today? That I haven't been on a horse since last fall? I won't be able to sit down for a week! They did all seem interested, but I don't know if they'll come or not."

Mrs. Day and I made big preparations for the party. She sent to Cheyenne for lemons. We couldn't get any ice, but the well water was cold enough for making lemonade. We each carried a bucket of water, brooms, mops, and dust cloths down to the school and gave it a good cleaning. We washed the windows, cleaned the blackboards, and polished the stove so it looked very nice.

Mrs. Day and I each baked a cake the morning of the party. Hers came out beautiful as always. I made a white cake, put pink coloring in it, and covered it with pink icing. It looked lovely, but when we cut it, the coloring had all gone to the bottom, so that it shaded from

---

3   Women's clubs were widespread during the late nineteenth and early twentieth centuries. Both urban and rural women gathered to discuss literature, housekeeping, and even social issues. In the early 1900s, rural women's clubs were promoted by *Wallaces Farmer*, an Iowa farm newspaper, and by Laura Ingalls Wilder, writing for the *Missouri Ruralist*. See John J. Fry, *The Farm Press, Reform, and Rural Change, 1895–1920* (New York: Routledge, 2005), 55–56 and Mildred White Wells, *Unity in Diversity: The History of the General Federation of Women's Clubs* (Washington, DC: General Federation of Women's Clubs, 1953).

white on top to red at the bottom of each layer. It was a most peculiar-looking cake.

Mrs. Day and I hustled through our noonday meal and were down at the schoolhouse at one o'clock. We figured the women would come early so that they could get home in time to get supper for their families. We took plates and glasses for twenty, figuring that some women would bring their children. We got everything ready, cut the cake, and made a gallon of lemonade.

We waited.

Mrs. Caster was the first to come, bringing small James. "I left Osa to bake the bread," she said. "I just hope she doesn't burn it." She admired our cleaning job. We sat down and talked about the stock and the wheat crop. These were important things to all of us.

Mrs. Gillaspie came bringing her youngest child. She'd walked a mile from the south. She was a bit shy, but we hashed over the wheat crop again and the stock, which was doing well on the grass.

"I wish we had a well," she said. "It takes a lot of time to go down to the creek for the water every day. We have so much washing with the children."

There wasn't a word of complaint about the hard task for her when Elvy was away working and she had to go to the creek, dip out pails of water, empty it into barrels on the wagon, and haul it home. "We just can't afford to have a well drilled yet. Elvy is down working in Colorado now. We've got two cows fresh, so we have plenty of milk for the children. I could sell some butter if I had any way to get it to Chugwater."

"I'd like to have some chickens," I said. "I always seem to be short of eggs, and we could use them instead of meat."

"We've got more hens than we need," Mrs. Gillaspie said. "I'll have to talk to Elvy, but I think we could sell you some. Maybe two dozen."

Mrs. Cline and Mrs. Derby came together. They had walked from their homes a mile to the west.[4] We talked over the good-looking stand of wheat and all the new calves. Mrs. Whittle came driving along the big, beautiful draft mares in the lumber wagon. Her oldest girl was about twelve. She was caring for the other five children at their home. Mrs. Whittle had a very decided Cockney brogue, and talked extremely fast. But we understood that their cow had dropped a calf the day before. It was a heifer, and that was important when everybody wanted to increase their stock.

"Now the kids can have milk again," she said simply. "I would have been here sooner, but one of our mares jumped the fence into the wheat field, and I had to chase her home. I never saw a mare that could jump like she can."

Mrs. Day and I looked at each other. It was after two o'clock. "I guess all the other women are too busy to come today," I said.

"Most likely the men wouldn't let 'em have a team or wouldn't bring 'em," Mrs. Caster said. "Seems like some of the men wants their women to stay at home and not go nowheres."

Undaunted, Mrs. Day broached the idea of regular meetings of the women every two weeks in the summer. There was silence.

Finally Mrs. Caster said timidly, "I don't know as I could get away every two weeks. Seems like there's so much work in the summer, and I've got to work in the garden. We put a lot of beans up at the edge of the wheat, and I know I'll have to do all the hoeing there." It was a long speech from her.

---

4   Lara Cline is listed in the 1920 US Census as living in the neighborhood. She and her husband John were both born in Iowa and they had one daughter. Edith C. Derby was the wife of Ray S. Derby, who homesteaded near the Clines (1910, 1920, and 1930 US Censuses, www.ancestry.com, accessed August 10, 2010; Tract records, Laramie County Clerk's Office, Cheyenne, Wyoming).

Mrs. Cline and Mrs. Derby said nothing. Mrs. Gillaspie agreed with Mrs. Caster. "Seems like I'm working all the time, and I'm too tired to walk this far if I ever get done with my work," she said.

"Well, if that's the way you feel about it," said Mrs. Day rather tartly, "the other women who live farther away will probably feel the same. We thought it would be nice to get together during the summer and visit when we don't have church or anything."

We served the cake and lemonade. There was plenty for seconds and thirds, which we urged on them. My pink cake was good for a laugh, but it tasted just as good as if it had been a delicate pink all the way through, the way I had intended.

Mrs. Whittle was the first to leave, and she offered Mrs. Gillaspie a ride. They swung the horses away from the hitching post and went galloping down the road in a swirl of dust. Mrs. Derby and Mrs. Cline said they'd had a nice time, and left walking slowly to the west. Mrs. Caster waited and helped us gather up the dishes and the remains of the cakes and lemonade. We closed the schoolhouse, and all three of us trudged up the road toward home, carrying the funeral meats. Of course our men teased us.[5]

---

5 The Days and Smiths had small households and were doing the absolute minimum necessary to fulfill homestead requirements. By contrast, their neighbors had to feed larger families with food they raised themselves. It is therefore not entirely surprising that this attempt at a women's club was stillborn.

Chapter Twenty-One

The Preacher on the Prairie

THERE WAS NO CHURCH OR SUNDAY SCHOOL ANYWHERE IN OUR AREA, so Mrs. Day suggested that we hold a Protracted Meeting[1] at our schoolhouse in the hope that enough interest would be aroused to have either preaching or Sunday school classes regularly. One young minister came out on a scouting trip to see whether we wanted church services. But when Mrs. Day found out that he was a Presbyterian, a different denomination than she was, she would have none of him. Immediately she wrote to the Home Missionary Board of her own Disciples of Christ Church and made arrangements for them to send us a minister from that board.[2]

This chap arrived in Chugwater on the train one morning. Nobody knew he was coming, so there was no one there to meet

---

1   A "protracted meeting" was a series of Christian worship services held on successive evenings. It was often called a revival or a camp meeting. Camp meetings originated during the Second Great Awakening of the early 1800s. They were common in many Protestant churches during the nineteenth and early twentieth centuries, but have become less popular since the 1960s. See Daniel G. Reid, et al., eds., *Dictionary of Christianity in America* (Downers Grove, IL: InterVarsity, 1990), 1013–1014; and Charles E. Hambrick-Stowe, *Charles G. Finney and the Spirit of American Evangelicalism* (Grand Rapids, MI: Eerdmans, 1996), 114–115.

2   Americans' attachment to particular denominations has historically been deep-seated, although this loyalty had weakened significantly after World War II. The Disciples of Christ had divided from the Presbyterians during the early 1800s. See Stow Persons, *American Minds: A History of Ideas* (New York: Holt, Rinehart, and Winston, 1958), 163–172; Alan Petigny, *The Permissive Society: America, 1941–1965* (New York: Cambridge, 2009), 60–70; and Edwin Scott Gaustad, *A Religious History of America*, New Revised Ed. (San Francisco: Harper & Row, 1990), 138–139.

him. He stood there on the platform with his baggage, looking off across the prairie in all directions with no idea where to go or what to do. The station agent directed him to the headquarters of Swan Land and Cattle Company, which was only a short distance away. There he explained his plight.

"I'm Paxton Graham from the Missionary Board," he told the manager. "I was sent out here to hold a Protracted Meeting at the Caster Schoolhouse, but nobody came to meet me."

"That's about twenty miles from here," said the manager. "We'll let you have a horse and you can return him when you leave." The young minister looked a bit flustered.

"But I've never ridden a horse before," Graham demurred. "That's a pretty long trip."

"We'll give you a gentle horse," the manager promised. "Bob, you saddle Dusty up for Reverend Graham." In a few minutes Bob brought out the horse saddled and bridled. Reverend Graham eyed the horse dubiously.

"How will I ever find my way for twenty miles?" he worried. "Is there a good road?"

"Well, I know there's a trail part of the way," said Bob. "But I don't guess you'd hardly call it a road. You follow that trail there along the railroad for a ways, and then it swings to the left and you keep on it. You just keep going south and west and you'll see some houses. Anybody over there can tell you where to go."

Then the cowboy cautioned, "There's just one thing about this horse, Dusty. He's scared of trains. If a train comes along, you keep the reins tight and you watch him. Aw, you'll be all right. There aren't no trains along at this time of day, unless it's a freight," he assured the perturbed-looking preacher.

Graham awkwardly climbed onto the horse and checked the small bundle of clothing which he'd tied on behind the saddle. He clucked to the horse, shook the reins gently, and Dusty ambled off in the direction pointed out, to the trail along the railroad track.

"Boss, do you figger that Dusty will be comin' back alone in a little while?" Bob asked the manager.

"Well, if he just gets away from the railway before that morning freight comes along, he'll be fine. But you know how Dusty hates to go faster than a walk. I suppose that preacher can surely ride a horse that'll walk."

Dusty plodded along at a slow pace for a mile or so down the trail by the railroad tracks, and Reverend Graham began to feel somewhat at ease. Suddenly on the bright morning air came the shattering blast of a train whistle. Dusty stepped up a bit. The whistle grew increasingly louder. Then Graham could plainly hear the train clacking toward him. But the trail still followed along the railroad track.

Graham's only thought was that if he should be thrown off the horse, his glasses would certainly be broken and he couldn't see to read without them. He tied the reins together, put them around his neck, and stuffed his glasses into his pocket just as the train came thundering by.

Dusty gave one buck and ran. Somehow Graham managed to hang onto the saddle and keep his feet in the stirrups. Dusty took off across that prairie with the preacher hanging on for dear life. Finally, when they were well away from the railroad track, the horse slowed down to a walk.

The preacher stopped the horse and sat there in the saddle, shaking. He was undecided what he should do next. He swung Dusty around and headed back for the trail. He was afraid to make the horse go faster than a walk, though, so it was some six hours later when he reached our house. Dusty was in much better shape than his rider. Reverend Graham was so tired and shaken that he could scarcely get off the horse. He had wandered off his original course and had gone well over twenty miles, as near as we could figure. He had finally found his way by using the afternoon sun to guide him.

Earle took the horse and I invited Reverend Graham into the house. He told us with some pride of how he had saved his glasses and stuck on the horse. But when he told of tying the reins together and putting them around his neck, Earle exploded.

"Don't you realize that if you had been thrown off the horse he would have dragged you by the neck? You wouldn't have had a chance!"

"I d-d-didn't think of that," the poor man stuttered. He sat down suddenly. "I-I-I never thought of that. I just thought of saving my glasses. Could I have a glass of water, Mrs. Smith?" I hastened over to bring him some cold water.

We explained that he would sleep at our house, and showed him his bedroom. I should say "the" bedroom, as Earle and I would go back to the sanitary cot in the dining room downstairs. Mrs. Day planned to give Reverend Graham his meals, and Earle took him over there shortly. The poor man was so sore and lame and weary that he could hardly walk.

The story of the preacher's misadventures with the horse was entirely too good to keep. Earle went down to Casters' to tell them that we would have preaching the next evening at the schoolhouse, and of course he had to share the joke with them. In the country, where even the children rode horseback everywhere, such stupidity in handling a horse could scarcely be comprehended.

Chapter Twenty-Two

Protracted Meeting

The following morning, Dr. Day took Reverend Graham back to Chugwater, leading Dusty behind the buggy, to get the preacher's suitcase, hymn books, and other small items. Earle rode to the neighbors' to spread the word about the meeting.

While we were making our plans for the evening services, I said, "I'll play the organ the best I can, Reverend Graham. But I haven't tried an organ in more than ten years. Organs take a lot more footwork than a piano. I hope you can choose some simple hymns, and I hope that you will lead the singing, because I'm not much of a singer." He admitted that he couldn't sing much either.

I went down to the schoolhouse that afternoon to practice the hymns that he had chosen, but I wasn't much pleased with my efforts. I frequently forgot to pump the organ as I watched the music, and the sound would die out dolefully.

That evening we made our own little procession as we walked the half-mile down the road to the schoolhouse. Reverend Graham and Dr. Day carried the hymn books, and Mrs. Day carried a lantern. Earle pushed the baby carriage with Bertel and carried another lantern. I had a lamp in one hand and the lamp chimney in the other.

All the seats in the schoolhouse were filled by seven-thirty. Men and women squeezed behind the desks, the older boys stood along the walls, while the little ones sat on the floor in the aisles or in front of the platform.

We hung up the lanterns, put a table and lamp on the platform, placed my lamp on the organ, and everything was ready. Reverend Graham announced a hymn. I did remember that I had to pump with one foot and then the other, but it was hard going. I had to watch the music, play with both hands, and keep my feet going—as well as trying to sing. The preacher and I had a duet for the first stanza. A few people joined timidly in the refrain, and by the end of the fourth stanza we were all doing pretty well.

Reverend Graham gave a short prayer, announced another hymn which was familiar to nearly everybody, and we all did better. Then came the text and the sermon.

Our churches were yet another of the familiar roots from which we had all been torn. The tremendous change to a new land, our efforts to adjust ourselves to this new life, and to wrest a living from a reluctant soil had put every one of us in a frame of mind to appreciate outside help. We wanted a message of cheer and comfort and encouragement. We would have welcomed an assurance that the good Lord was on our side and that He would take some interest in our welfare.[1]

Instead, we had a sermon on some of the obscure doctrines of Reverend Graham's particular denomination, which left us bewildered and disappointed. The small children went to sleep. The older youngsters nodded; the adults listened with curious, baffled expressions. Finally the sermon was over and we had another prayer. The preacher announced another hymn. I was so weary that I couldn't keep my feet

---

1   Historians have noted the role of the church as a sociological and psychological anchor for rural people. See Robert P. Swierenga, "The Little White Church: Historiographical Revisions about Religion in Rural America," in *History and the Christian Historian*, edited by Ronald A. Wells (Grand Rapids, MI: Eerdmans, 1998), 159–177.

going, so the organ gave a dying gasp until I frantically pumped it up again and it came out with too much volume.

When the service was finally over, there were sighs of relief as everyone struggled out of the small school seats. They all looked tired. Fathers gathered up the little ones to carry them a mile or two home. Mothers wakened the older children and, grasping them firmly by the hand, started out for the long walk. A few loaded the youngsters onto lumber wagons and drove off across the prairie.

Our group was the last to leave. Our baby howled his dislike of riding in his go-cart over the rough road, so Earle had to carry him. I put the lamp into the baby carriage and pushed it. The preacher carried our lantern, and Dr. Day carried the other things.

Not a word was said about the sermon. Mrs. Day remarked, "I'm pleased that so many were here tonight. Nearly everybody who was close enough to come was on hand."

"It was a very attentive congregation," said Reverend Graham rather smugly.

We used the same hymns every night, and I became more used to pumping the organ, so the singing was somewhat louder—if not lusty. Reverend Graham spent his days visiting with Dr. Day or with Earle, writing poetry, and resting.

Yet this brash young preacher sent out by the Mission Board preached as though his audience were all college professors. It wasn't that his thoughts about the gospel were above our heads. But oh, how he loved polysyllables! I thought that he must have rewritten his sermons and substituted a longer word whenever he could find one. The meetings went on for two weeks. Each night there was a bit more hellfire and damnation, but never in simple words or homely phrases.

He had all of his sermons prepared, all of them on obscure doctrines or points of theology. This went on for about a week. Then one day, he returned to our house looking very crestfallen after having breakfast at Dr. Day's house.

"Mrs. Smith," he asked, "could I use this table in the living room for some work?"

"Surely," I answered. "I'll clear it off for you right now."

I was busy downstairs. Reverend Graham worked all morning, pacing the floor when he wasn't writing at the table. Immediately after lunch, he hurried upstairs and was up there alone all afternoon.

That night he used as his text the parable of the sower and the seed. He gave a good, down-to-earth talk. He prayed that the people assembled there might be prospered and their move to a new environment be blessed. There was more animation on the faces of the congregation than there had been the whole time he'd been there.

After that, Reverend Graham worked all day, every day, and delivered some very good sermons. At least they were suited to his audience. He still couldn't get away from using big words, and reminded me somewhat of my father in that respect. The last night of the meetings, in response to Reverend Graham's invitation, five of the teenagers requested to be admitted to the church.

It was a long time before Mrs. Day told me what had happened. She said, "I just couldn't stand those sermons any longer. Nobody understood what he was talking about, and it wasn't important anyway. I just said to him, 'Reverend Graham, you are not preaching the right kind of sermons for us. We care absolutely nothing for those fine points of doctrine and theology that you have been expounding. We want something more like old-time religion. But not hellfire and damnation.

"These neighbors are good people and doing the best they can. Don't you realize that all of us left our settled communities, our friends and relatives, to come out here to Wyoming? Younger people with families gave up everything familiar to them, their ways of farming and their way of life. They are worried about the future. They have been accustomed to gardens and fruit, milk and butter, and plenty of good food for the children. Here it is questionable if we can raise gardens, and we could certainly have no fruit. Just what are the mothers going to have for the children?'

"I was so indignant, I couldn't seem to stop. 'We would like to think that the Lord is here too; that he's interested in the well-being of all of us. Bless our work and help us make a living to develop this country so that the children will have a better future than they would have had back home.'

"He didn't have a word to say, but scooted back to your house. The rest of his sermons showed that he took what I said to heart." She chuckled. "Dr. Day thought I was a bit blunt, but I just couldn't help it. It was just too much to have the neighbors make the effort to come, and then be given a stone," she continued. "Mrs. Caster gets six children ready and walks half a mile. Mrs. Gillaspie brings her three children, and has to carry the smallest one more than a mile. The others walk a mile or two, and I couldn't stand it any longer to listen to those prepared sermons! He must have written them in the seminary," she snorted. [2]

———

Now that there were five converts, they would have to be baptized while the minister was there. Reverend Graham was firm in his belief that immersion was necessary, so the question was, where could we find enough water? In all sincerity, Earle offered the use of our concrete horse tank—which was new and clean—but Reverend Graham

---

2   In these paragraphs, Laura relates Mrs. Day's particular version of Christianity, a view that has been shared by many Americans. She desires preaching that is encouraging and traditional, but that does not stress sin or hell. She asks for it to be mainly future-minded and attuned to the conditions of the congregants. She did not desire to be challenged in her own beliefs or to have to work to understand the concepts presented. For a more-recent version of such a view of Christianity, see Christian Smith and Melinda Lundquist Denton, *Soul-Searching: The Religious and Spiritual Lives of American Teenagers* (New York: Oxford, 2005).

wanted running water. There was only one solution, and that was to find a spot in Chugwater Creek deep enough for immersion.

The next day, all of the congregation met at Diamond. There was quite a procession of wagons, top buggies, and boys on horseback. We found a pool of water in the creek that was about two and a half feet deep. All of us gathered on the bank.

Reverend Graham came out of the Diamond Railway Station wearing a suit with a frock coat. Years before it may have been black, but now it was a sad faded green, wrinkled and tight from many baptisms. The sleeves were short, and the trousers only went halfway to his knees.

"We will sing 'Shall We Gather at the River.' Mrs. Smith, will you lead the singing?" the preacher asked. I was so tickled at his absurd appearance that I could hardly keep from giggling. The children gazed at him in awe. I did manage to restrain myself and start the hymn. I pitched it too high, so we had to start over again. We'd sung this hymn every night during the meetings, so everyone joined in.

When the preacher led the first girl into the stream, she pulled back and squealed as he immersed her in the cold water. The second girl and the first two boys were tight-lipped, and didn't make a sound as he took them into the water. The four stood dripping and shivering in the chilly wind. Then came the third boy. He wasn't very well, and we noticed that he was shaking as he awaited his turn. Reverend Graham led him into the stream.

At that moment, we happened to notice the three little Caster boys and the two Gillaspies. Each one was hunkered down, picking up rocks. They were watching the proceedings with absorbed intentness. The preacher glanced up and saw them. Nobody could imagine what the boys were going to do with the rocks, but they certainly had their sights set on the two in the water.

Preacher Graham, completely unnerved, slipped and fell, dragging the wildly thrashing boy with him. The boys on the bank paid no attention to the struggle; they stood poised and watching. The preacher regained his feet and hauled the boy, still kicking and sputtering, out onto the bank. Instantly the other boys sent a barrage of rocks into the water exactly where the preacher had been. A water snake was swimming near the baptismal pool! All of us gasped in relief. There were nervous giggles as we tried to look properly solemn and sing one more hymn.

Reverend Graham dripped over to the railway station and disappeared inside. We never saw him again. Everybody loaded up and started for home. Earle and I laughed like a couple of idiots all the way.

Mrs. Day later left the Disciples of Christ Church and became a Presbyterian.[3]

---

3   This last piece of information was supplied by Earle to Alan Andersen in 1983 (Alan Andersen, telephone conversation with author, November 21, 2008).

CHAPTER TWENTY-THREE

Dance and Election

CHARLES ELMER LANE, OF CHEYENNE, WYOMING, WAS RUNNING FOR election on the Republican ticket.[1] He came out to get Earle to take him around the neighborhood. Earle was always interested in politics. He knew practically everybody for miles around, so he was more than ready to help. Mr. Lane arrived one morning in the summer, and they started off at once in Mr. Lane's Ford to make the rounds. When they returned late that afternoon they announced that our old friend Anderson had built a new barn, and everybody was invited to a dance over there that evening.

Mrs. Day offered to keep the baby when I went over to tell her about the dance. In fact, she insisted that a barn dance was no place to take a baby. So I agreed. She had never kept Bertel before, but he saw her every day and neither of us figured that there would be any difficulty. Earle and I hurried through supper and I dressed in my best for the party. By that time there was a road—or at least two tracks

---

1 Charles Elmer Lane was born in Cheyenne in 1878. He was secretary for Senator Francis E. Warren (see the footnote in chapter 1) from 1905 to 1912, and received his law degree from Georgetown Law School in 1911. In 1916, Lane was running for County and Prosecuting Attorney of Laramie County, but he lost the Republican Primary on August 22. However, he was subsequently elected to that post in 1918 and served until 1921. He later served in the Wyoming House of Representatives from 1927 to 1929 ("Gleason and Allison Both Win, According to Returns Last Night," *Cheyenne State Leader*, August 24, 1916; "Attorney Elmer Lane Dies," *Wyoming State Tribune*, June 16, 1964).

with a high center—which only a Ford could have negotiated without being hung up. Mr. Lane, Earle, and I drove over to Andersons' barn in Lane's car.

We arrived in good time. Several wagons were there, the horses unhitched and tied to the wheels, and a number of riding horses were tied to the wagons. There was a charge of twenty-five cents, which included sandwiches and coffee later. There was a good crowd.

We climbed to the second floor, which was the haymow, and I was surprised to see how many people were there. I sat down with some of the women I knew who were seated on plank seats along the side. The men were still lounging outside, so Earle took Mr. Lane down to meet them. He was after more votes. After all, electioneering was what we'd actually come for.

Presently, one old fellow with a fiddle and another with a guitar tuned up, and the men came scrambling up the stairs. I had never been allowed to dance when I was at home, and I had danced very little since then. But Mr. Lane insisted that he must have the first dance with me.

"But I don't dance, Mr. Lane," I protested.

"Oh, come on. This is just a square dance, and the caller will tell you what to do." Mr. Lane probably couldn't imagine a young girl who actually didn't know how to dance. But he didn't know my strict Methodist parents.

"Come on, Mrs. Smith," he said. "There's just one place left in that set." So, much against my better judgment, I hustled over with him to complete the group. I had played Skip to My Lou and all those sorts of games, so I figured I could get through some way. The fiddle and guitar started out with a square dance. That wasn't so bad. They kept a good rhythm, and I could follow fairly well just from the party games I had been playing years before. I knew how to do-si-do and allemande left, and it was simple enough to be swung. I managed very well. I wasn't lost any oftener than some of the others.[2]

The men particularly liked to whirl their partners. I weighed about one hundred pounds, and it seemed to me my feet were off the floor most of the time. I was really starting to have fun. Then came a grand-right-and-left the whole length of the barn. I was too busy to notice that at the end of the line the men twirled their partners with special enthusiasm. When my turn came, my partner gave me a tremendous whirl and somehow let loose of me.

My feet slipped and I sprawled flat on the floor. My partner was a big man. He picked me up, mumbled something about being sorry, and we both went on through the right-and-left. I was furious and terribly embarrassed. I pretended to think it was funny, as everyone else did, but I was seething. I wish I'd have carried a hat pin; I'd have stuck that big oaf. Being five-foot-two and slender, I always had double my share of trouble when it came to swing-your-partner. There was nothing I could do about it but say, "Let me down, let me down!"

Mr. Lane tried to get me to dance again later, but I was too mortified. I simply could not do it. I spent the rest of the evening talking to the older women.

Then, after our sandwiches and coffee, we left for home. It was the first time I had been away from home after dark. The prairie was too big for us, and it would have been easy to get lost, so we had always managed to get home before dark. With the headlights on the Ford, it

---

2   For a brief history of square dancing, see S. Foster Damon, *The History of Square Dancing* (Barre, MA: Barre Gazette, 1957); a contemporary explanation of square-dance moves is found in Dudley Laufman and Jacqueline Laufman, *Traditional Barn Dances with Calls and Fiddling* (Champaign, IL: Human Kinetics, 2009).

was no trick at all to follow the road. We were home in an unbelievably short time.[3]

There we found the baby screaming and Mrs. Day exhausted. "He woke up about half an hour after you left, and he's cried most of the time since," she said wearily. That didn't help my low spirits any to think she'd had to put up with such an evening.

By the fall of 1916, Bertel was old enough to toddle along after Earle as he went about, doing his chores. One day, not long before Earle was to return to Fort Madison to teach, Bert followed Earle out to the barn. Earle had just gotten Bill out of the stable and was going to take the bar down—when he dropped it. Bill lurched sideways and knocked Bert down senseless.

When Earle turned, he saw Bill's hoof hanging over Bert's head. He said, "Bill, stand still!" Bill was a spirited horse, but he knew what had happened. He didn't move a foot till Earle got Bert out of the way. Of course, Earle took Bert over to Dr. Day right away and he was all right.

When Election Day came that fall, Dr. Day loaded Mrs. Day, myself, and the baby into the lumber wagon and drove us over to the Robinson School eight miles away to vote. It was cold and snowing a little. Dr. Day wore his derby hat, and I was tickled. There he was, perched up on the spring seat of a lumber wagon, wearing a derby hat. He didn't look funny; he looked dignified. That was the kind of hat he preferred, and he wore it, cold or not.

---

3   Although this chapter is the first place that Laura mentions a car, Wyoming had numerous automobiles by the 1910s. Many of the first cars in Wyoming counties were owned by sheep ranchers. For homesteaders with less resources, cars would have been less common. Registration of motor vehicles was first required in Wyoming in 1913. See Phil Roberts, et al., eds., *Wyoming Almanac*, 5th edition, revised (Laramie, WY: Skyline West, 2001), 71–77; Larson, *History of Wyoming*, 344–345.

That was the first election in which I ever voted. For the first time since Wyoming had become a state in 1890, women were allowed the right to vote. Mrs. Day was delighted. Wyoming had given women suffrage in their state constitution, so we could vote in 1916, four years before other states allowed women to vote. Mrs. Day and I felt very important as we marked our ballots and stuffed them into the slit in a dry-goods box. I think we canceled each other's votes, but still we had the privilege of voting.[4]

---

4   Voting in this election, four years before the Nineteenth Amendment to the Constitution gave the vote to all women in the United States (including Iowa), must have made a significant impression on Laura. However, her descriptions here are incorrect; 1916 was not the first time that women in Wyoming could vote. In fact, Wyoming Territory first gave women the vote for all offices, and the ability to serve in all offices, in 1869. When Wyoming became a state in 1890, it continued the practice. See T. A. Larson, *Wyoming: A Bicentennial History* (New York: Norton, 1977), 76–107.

Epilogue

EARLE WAS PRINCIPAL OF JEFFERSON SCHOOL AT FORT MADISON during the fall of 1916. I stayed until our seven months were up. We had completed our time; the three years were finished! I joined Earle at Fort Madison.

In December 1916, Earle went back to Wyoming alone to "prove up." He had filed on the homestead in April of 1913. We had gone out to live there the following August. We had to have two witnesses, so Dr. Day and Luther Caster were there in Cheyenne with Earle when he got title to our land in 1916.

Earle had received a telegram that fall informing us he had passed the Civil Service Examination for the Philippines, and had been given an appointment there. So we were soon busy making plans for that next adventure in our lives.

———

We kept our ranch in Wyoming for over fifty years and rented it out on shares. For thirty of those years, we rented it to Clyde Caster, one of Luther's younger sons, who married Roy Duvall's daughter and still lives near the Caster Ranch. He has been very successful, and has bought many of the surrounding ranches. He now owns five thousand acres.

Dr. Day and Jessie moved to Fairfield, Iowa, and lived there for the rest of their lives. Luther and Ethel Caster also moved back to Moravia; Ethel never could stand the wind out in Wyoming.

Herschel Sells moved to Cheyenne to work. One day a freight elevator fell on him. He was so strong that he was able to hold the elevator up, but he strained himself terribly and never recovered from that injury.

Elvy Gillaspie was a n'er-do-well, and spent his days poaching pronghorn deer. Old Dave Gillaspie ran a blacksmith shop out of his shack until he died.

In 1936, Earle developed a severe case of appendicitis and nearly died. We went back out to Wyoming, fixed up our old house, bought a wind-charger,[1] and spent the summer at the old homestead. It really did us both good.

---

1   A wind-charger is a windmill connected to a generator so that the house had electricity for lights and appliances. Electric wires were not run to the house on the homestead until the 1980s.

Afterword

by John J. Fry

I FREQUENTLY TELL MY STUDENTS THAT HISTORY IS MORE FASCINATING than fiction. Often what actually happened in the past could never have been thought of by a novelist. This is true of the improbable life of Benjamin Franklin, the fifteenth child (and tenth son) of a New England candlemaker and soapmaker. By the end of his life, Benjamin had become enormously wealthy, met both the kings of France and of England, and negotiated an alliance with France that enabled the thirteen American colonies to win the Revolutionary War.[1] It is also true of Woodrow Wilson, the stubborn son of a southern Presbyterian pastor who was elected president of the United States barely fifty years after his region had voted to leave the country. As president, he would rather have had the Treaty of Versailles voted down than to have it passed without his masterpiece, the League of Nations.[2] Again and again, history depicts men and women acting in ways that are idiosyncratic, surprising, and remarkable. As a result, the discipline remains engaging, entertaining, and educational.

What is true of founding fathers and presidents is also often true of ordinary Americans. It would be difficult to make up the life of Earle and Laura Smith. Born in small towns in south-central Iowa, they ultimately lived in a variety of places. After homesteading in Wyoming, Earle taught briefly in the Philippine Islands, served as

---

1   Gordon Wood, *The Americanization of Benjamin Franklin* (New York: Penguin, 2004).

2   David M. Kennedy, *Over Here: The First World War and American Society* (New York: Oxford, 1980), 357–362; Paul Johnson, *A History of the American People* (New York: HarperCollins, 1997), 648–656.

a county attorney, and worked for the Iowa state government. They moved to Florida in retirement, but then they returned to Iowa several years later. Their relentless pursuit of opportunity took them across the country and around the world. Their mobility was shared by Americans throughout the history of the United States. Many contemporary readers may find a bit of their own life story in that of the Smiths'.

In the footnotes, I have attempted to provide some immediate context for the places, people, and events that Laura mentions. This afterword will also share some broader contexts for *Almost Pioneers*. I will argue that the best ways to understand Laura Gibson Smith are as an Iowan, as a Western woman writer, as a visitor to Wyoming and the West, and as an American. Thus, I will first locate the book in Laura and Earle's life stories and describe how the manuscript came to be written. Then, I will discuss how Laura's account exhibits the characteristics of a woman's view of living in the American West. Third, I will address how their time in Wyoming intersects with the history of the state and the history of the West, offering some observations about two visits I took to the homestead. Finally, I will consider how their story fits into broader narratives of the history of the United States.

Laura and Earle were both Iowans. Earle Sloan Smith was born in Anita, Iowa, on November 11, 1890. The 1890 census listed Anita as a town of 695. Anita is in the northeast corner of Cass County, about sixty-five miles almost due west of Des Moines. His father, Frank R. Smith, was from Kewanee, Illinois, and his mother, Dora B. Smith, was born in Iowa of parents who were from Ohio. When Earle applied for a passport in 1917, he listed his father as still living in the United States, but he had no more details to provide. It appears that Frank either abandoned his family or obtained a divorce from Dora, which was difficult but not impossible in Iowa at the turn of the twentieth century. At any rate, when the census-taker caught up with young Earle, it was in the town of Ames in 1910. His mother Dora had remarried, as he noted in the foreword. The new head of the household was Adelbert B. Maxwell. Other family members included Lula Smith, who was twenty-seven; Laura Smith, who was twenty-three (and is mentioned briefly in chapter 17); Earle, who was nineteen; and Mildred Maxwell, who was twenty-three.[3] One can only wonder what life was like for a nineteen-year-old male with four adult women in that house in Ward 1 of Ames.

Laura Blanche Gibson was born two and a half months after Earle, on January 24, 1891. She was born in the rural community of Marne, Iowa, in the northwest corner of Cass County, about eighty-five miles from Des Moines and about twenty miles west of Anita. Her mother Josephine had been born in Illinois to parents from New England; her father was born in New York, and her mother in Connecticut. Laura's father was born in Scotland. Marne in 1890 was a town of 350 people. In 1900, however, the Gibson family was in Clay Township in Shelby County, Iowa, just northwest of Cass County. Laura's parents had been married thirty-four years in 1900, and her mother had given birth to eleven children. Ten were still alive. Laura's father was born in 1832 and her mother in 1846, making him sixty-seven and her fifty-three in 1900.[4] Like Earle, Laura was the youngest child in her family, although her family was quite a bit larger. Just as one might speculate

---

3   Iowa Genealogical Society, County Research Guides: "15. Cass County, Iowa," www.iowa genealogy.org/CountyResearchGuide/CassCoGuide.htm, accessed June 14, 2010; 1910 US Census, 1917 Passport Application, www.ancestry.com, accessed March 6, 2008.

4   Iowa Genealogical Society, "15. Cass County, Iowa," accessed June 14, 2010; 1900 and 1910 US Censuses, www.ancestry.com, accessed March 6, 2008.

about Earle and the women in his household, one might ponder how Laura got along with her nine older brothers and sisters, and whether that was partially why she and Earle had only one child during their sixty-two years of marriage.

For some reason, both families relocated to Ames after 1900. From Earle's foreword, it appears that Laura's family moved to their home in Ward 2 from California in the summer or fall of 1907. Earle's family was already living in town. Both Earle and Laura attended Ames High School. Together they were two-thirds of the Ames High School debate team in 1908–09. The front-page article in the *Ames Times* mentioned in the foreword is from January 28, 1909. The headline is HIGH SCHOOL DEBATERS WHO HAVE WON TWO BIG VICTORIES, and it features pictures of Laura, Earle, and Homer Templeton. The story describes their victory over debate teams from Winterset and Bedford, Iowa. In fact, the Ames team had won all of their matches that year. On February 26, they traveled to Fremont County to debate the team from Tabor High School for the championship of the Southwest District of Iowa. Unfortunately, Homer Templeton was stricken by the measles the day before the contest and was unable to participate. Their team lost the debate, two judges to one.[5]

Earle graduated from Ames High School on June 3, 1909, and delivered the class oration at commencement. The reporter for the *Ames Times* described it this way:

> *The class oration was in the hands of Ames high school peerless enuncia-tor, Earle Smith. Earle in common with others on the program showed a slight lack of preparation. He made a few hesitations, a thing we have*

5 "High School Debaters Who Have Won Two Big Victories," *Ames Times*, January 28, 1909; "Girl Debaters of Tabor are Battling for State Honors," *Ames Times*, February 25, 1909; "Big Debate is Friday Night," *Ames Times*, February 25, 1909; "Ames Lost to Tabor Girls," *Ames Times*, March 4, 1909.

never seen him do before, but his rendering of Bryant's immortal lines
from "Thanatopsis," "So live that when thy summons come to join the
innumerable caravan," etc. was excellent. His delivery was good and the
old words inspired, something they seldom do in the mouth of a novice.[6]

Laura graduated a year later almost to the day, on June 2, 1910.
During her senior year, Ames High School had two debate teams, but
Laura was not on either one. She did act in the senior class play, *At*
the Sign of the Jack-o-Lantern. The *Ames Times* noted that "Laura Gibson as Mrs. Smithers, Clyde Griffith as Richard Chester, and Neville
Noble as Eloise St. Clair deserve special mention." When the *Times*
printed that year's list of graduates and what they planned to do after
commencement, it listed "College or teach" for Laura.[7]

Earle picks up the narrative here, and the book describes their
years together in the mid-1910s. As has been noted in the footnote to
the passage in the foreword, Earle and Laura were indeed married in
Chicago on July 24, 1911. They most likely did intend to keep their
marriage a secret for a while. The idea was not unheard of in the area,
for two *Ames Times* articles in 1909 and 1911 described secret marriages. One couple had been married in Kalamazoo, Michigan, nearly
a year before the bride told her family or friends in Story County. The
other had been married in Chicago several months before the news
broke. It is entirely possible that their cover was blown by a reporter
for a Chicago newspaper who knew them from Ames. Unfortunately,

---

6   "Ames H.S. Class Day Exercises," *Ames Times*, June 3, 1909. "Thanatopsis," by William Cullen
    Bryant (1794–1878) was first published in 1821. *Thanatopsis* means a view of death. Bryant's
    poem was a staple of public school education well into the twentieth century (Albert F.
    McLean Jr., "Bryant's 'Thanatopsis': A Sermon in Stone," *American Literature* 31[4], January
    1960, 474–479).

7   "The Two Ames High School Debate Teams," *Ames Times*, March 10, 1910; "The Class Play
    was Well Rendered," *Ames Times*, April 28, 1910; "H.S. Students Form Plans," *Ames Times*,
    June 9, 1910.

I have been unable to find the announcement mentioned in the foreword in any Des Moines newspaper.[8]

There is a slight tension in the narrative over whether Earle and Laura ever intended to remain on the homestead. When one first reads the book, it dawns somewhat slowly that Laura and Earle were not going to stay in Wyoming. It is clear from chapter 1 that they moved to Wyoming to obtain land. Later, in chapter 12, it becomes evident that they were doing the absolute minimum necessary to get title. In chapter 17, their conversation with Laura's mother indicates that they had come to the conviction that row-crop farming in the area would not be successful. Their final decision is not described explicitly until chapter 20. Still, Earle never did the farm work himself; he paid someone to plow the necessary acreage and then allowed someone else to grow crops on it in a share agreement. He mainly made money from teaching and spent it on homesteading. While in the early chapters one may assume that they were planning to stay, Laura doesn't really ever say that they were. It seems likely to me that they never meant to move to Wyoming permanently. I believe that they always had Earle's law school in mind, and saw obtaining property that could be leased to someone else as a step toward that goal.

After "proving up" on the homestead in December 1916, Laura, Earle, and Bertel returned to Fort Madison, Iowa, but this was only to prepare for another sojourn in an even more foreign land. As the epilogue notes, Earle had taken and passed the civil service exam for service in the Philippine Islands. From 1917 to 1920, Earle taught at a school run by the United States government in Iloilo, the capital of Iloilo province in the Philippines. While there, Earle volunteered to fight in World War I, but he was stationed in the Philippines for the duration of the war, and he went back to teaching when the war ended.

8   Marriage License, July 24, 1911, Cook County Vital Records, Chicago, Illinois. " 'I'm Married Now' Said She," *Ames Times*, November 11, 1909; "Another Nevada Pipe Dream," *Ames Times*, March 16, 1911.

The family resettled in Ames in 1920 and lived there until 1923, when Earle accepted another contract to teach in Iloilo. This time the family only lived there two years. They again settled in Ames in 1925.[9] One might piece together a description and narrative of the Smiths' life in the Philippines (which is beyond the scope of this book) from diaries and short stories that Laura wrote while they lived there. These materials are available at the Iowa Women's Archives at the University of Iowa in Iowa City.

In 1926, Earle again can be found in the public records when he ran as a Republican for Story County Attorney. He was nominated by the Republican primary in June, and won the general election unopposed on November 8.[10] Apparently, Earle had attended law school when the family was in the United States, from 1920 to 1923. He earned his bachelor's degree in law from the Chattanooga College of Law in 1921. The Chattanooga College was a law school in Tennessee that was not accredited by the American Bar Association. He must have passed the examination for the Iowa Bar during the early 1920s in order to run for county attorney. He served in this capacity from 1926 to 1930.[11]

Sometime during the 1930s, the Smiths moved to Des Moines. It may be that the Depression made it difficult for Republicans hoping to be elected in Story County. Alternatively, perhaps the Smiths moved to Des Moines simply to pursue greater opportunity for his

---

9   "Another Anita Boy," newspaper clipping in Laura Gibson Smith Papers, Box 2, Earle Sloan Smith Folder, and Laura Gibson Smith Papers, Box 1, Journals, April–May 1925, Iowa Women's Archives, Iowa City, Iowa.

10 Primary Election Record, Story County, Iowa, June 1926; Minutes of the Board of Supervisors of Story County, June 15, 1926, November 9, 1926; all available at Story County Courthouse, Nevada, Iowa.

11 Edgar Rubey Harlan, ed., *A Narrative History of the People of Iowa* (Chicago: American Historical Society, 1931), Vol. 1; *Catalogue and Announcement of the Chattanooga College of Law* (Chattanooga: Chattanooga College of Law, 1922); W. Raymond Blackard, "Law Schools in Tennessee," *The Tennessee Law Review* 14 (1936), 267–271; Stephen H. Holmes, Story County Attorney, letter to the author, August 6, 2010.

legal practice. In 1940, *Polk's Des Moines City Directory* lists Earle as a lawyer there. He and Laura were living in an apartment on Sixteenth Street.[12] The next year, the city directory lists him as working as an auditor for the State Tax Commission, and the couple's address as a different apartment on Nineteenth Street. Between 1940 and 1957, the city directory lists Earle's occupation as a series of different positions for the State Tax Commission: counsel, department director, director of retail sales and use tax, and state gasoline tax collector. In 1956 the Drake Law School Alumni Directory listed his position as counsel, Division of Special Taxes, State Tax Commission. City directories also indicate that the Smiths moved to a house on East Thirty-Seventh Street sometime between 1947 and 1949. Neither Smith is listed in the city directory after 1957.[13]

The Smiths retired to Tavares, Florida, sometime after 1957. Tavares is a small town nestled between several lakes about thirty-five miles northwest of Orlando.[14] They were still living there in 1971,[15] but it appears that they moved back to Des Moines sometime during the next two years. Laura died in 1973 and was buried in the Ames Municipal Cemetery. Earle then relocated to Ames, where he lived another twelve years. He died a few months before his ninety-fifth birthday, in 1985, and was laid to rest next to Laura. Their son Bertel died two years later at age seventy-four; he is also in the family burial plot at the edge of the cemetery, overlooking farmland in the South Skunk River valley.

Born and buried in the Hawkeye State, Laura and Earle were

---

12 *Polk's Des Moines City Directory, 1940* (Omaha: R. L. Polk, 1940), 748.

13 *Polk's Des Moines City Directory, 1941*; *Polk's Des Moines City Directory, 1942*; *Polk's Des Moines City Directory, 1944*; *Polk's Des Moines City Directory, 1946*; *Polk's Des Moines City Directory, 1949*; *Polk's Des Moines City Directory, 1957*. All were published in Omaha by the R. L. Polk publishing company.

14 City of Tavares, "Tavares: America's Seaplane City," www.tavares.org/, accessed June 23, 2010.

15 Laura Gibson Smith Papers, Box 1, Journals, January–December 1971, Iowa Women's Archives, Iowa City, Iowa.

both essentially lifelong Iowans. Their brief sojourns in Wyoming, the Philippines, and Florida only serve to underscore this fact. As a result, they were only visitors in Wyoming. However, their time there made a significant impact on their life, providing both ongoing economic support and a collection of vibrant memories. Laura later wrote about her experience in Wyoming, becoming one of many Western women writers.

⌐ ⌐

I do not know if Laura Smith kept a diary or journal when she and Earle homesteaded in Wyoming. It may be that she did, since some of the events are described in painstaking detail. I also do not know when she wrote *Almost Pioneers*. From internal and external evidence, it appears that she at least waited until after the 1930s. Internally, the epilogue mentions their return to the homestead in 1936. Chapter 12 also mentions that the porch roof of the house stayed on for forty years. If this is taken literally, then it would mean that she was writing after 1954. In addition, her comments in chapter 19—that baby clothing "now" was much simpler than it was in 1915—suggests that some amount of time had elapsed. Externally, the Federal Writers' Project published *Wyoming: A Guide to Its History, Highways, and People* in 1941. As mentioned in the footnote in chapter 4, the description of how Chugwater got its name was taken word for word from that publication.[16] I surmise that the earliest Laura could have written the manuscript is the middle of the 1940s. It is more likely that she didn't begin writing it until the 1950s. By this stage of their life, they had settled into a house in Des Moines, and Earle had a steady job in state government. Laura would have been in her sixties and may have wanted to save her memories in more-permanent form, and to share them with others.

---

16   *Wyoming: A Guide to Its History, Highways, and People*, 291.

Some other examples of Laura's writing have been preserved. As has been mentioned, some short stories and essays about life in the Philippines and the family's years there are available at the Iowa Women's Archives.[17] It does not appear that any of these were published, although she did send a short story to *The Farmer's Wife*, a farm newspaper published in St. Paul, Minnesota, in 1931. The rejection letter reads:

Dear Mrs. Smith: Your short story, "Interest Money," interests us very much even though we cannot consider buying it. We are over-supplied with manuscripts and therefore we are practically "off of the market." How long we will be "off," we cannot say now. However, we wish that you would keep our needs in mind and let us hear from you again later.[18]

One has to assume that the exigencies of the Great Depression were involved in the newspaper's oversupply. Unfortunately, the manuscript for this short story did not survive.

From my reading of some of Laura's journals, I believe that she must have edited her material about their life in Wyoming, perhaps several times. It doesn't sound like her journal entries, which are more episodic, more impressionistic, and more like diary entries. The chapters in *Almost Pioneers* have a firm narrative thrust. Laura evidently meant for these stories to be shared, although it's not clear how widely she hoped to share them. Perhaps it was just for her family and close acquaintances; perhaps she did have some idea of broader publication.

In 1983, ten years after Laura's death, Laura and Earle's son

---

17   Laura Gibson Smith Papers, Box 2, Short Stories Folder, Iowa Women's Archives, Iowa City, Iowa.

18   F. W. Beckman, letter to Laura G. Smith, December 30, 1931, Laura Gibson Smith Papers, Box 2, Short Stories Folder, Iowa Women's Archives, Iowa City, Iowa.

Bertel—everyone called him Bert—contacted Alan Andersen, executive editor of Life Story Enterprises, a small firm in Ankeny, Iowa. Andersen and a partner formed the company to collect stories and print bound volumes for families that wanted to preserve their history. They used recording equipment to interview family members and then assembled their life stories in narrative form. In the case of *Almost Pioneers,* Laura had already written a complete manuscript, but there were multiple versions of a few chapters. Alan assembled the final book from these drafts. He also did some interviews with Earle to fill in some missing pieces, most notably the foreword, the account of the buggy ride to Cheyenne at the end of chapter 18, and the last sentence of chapter 22. Andersen then typed the manuscript and had about a dozen copies printed and bound. These copies were given by Bert to family members and friends. I am indebted to Alan for his work on the manuscript. Apparently, he returned all of the Smiths' materials to Bert, including the different versions of the stories that Laura had written.[19]

Bert had been married for a number of years to Mabel Smith, but they had no children. In about 1970, he married a second time. Bernice Evelyn Wheatcraft had two grown sons, Michael and William. Bert died in 1987, and the next year, Michael and his wife Cathy moved into Bert's house in West Des Moines. There they found a box of written materials in the basement containing the bound manuscript and some of Laura's journals and pictures. In 1992, the Iowa Women's Archives was founded at the University of Iowa. Its mission was to preserve and make available documents and artifacts about the experiences of Iowa women. To obtain materials, the Archives ran advertisements in Iowa newspapers asking for donations. Cathy contacted the

---

19   Michael Wheatcraft and Cathy Wheatcraft, conversation with author, March 19, 2008; Alan Andersen, telephone conversation with author, November 21, 2008.

Archives and eventually donated this box of materials. Unfortunately, Laura's earlier drafts were not in the box that the Wheatcrafts found. As a result, they were not donated, and family members doubt that they still exist.[20]

I first encountered the manuscript in the fall of 2000. I was in the midst of feverishly researching what Midwestern farmers and their families were reading at the turn of the twentieth century for my dissertation, which later became my first book.[21] Reading *Almost Pioneers* in the Iowa Women's Archives made me slow down, enjoy, and laugh out loud at times. I commented to Kären Mason, the director of the Archives, that someone should get the manuscript published. After I had finished the first book, I contacted Kären to see if anyone had spoken to her about doing just that. She said no, and she provided me with Cathy Wheatcraft's phone number. Cathy and the other Wheatcrafts were happy to support my idea, so I proceeded.

In addition to her identity as an Iowan, Laura Smith was also a woman who wrote about her experience in the West. When she sat down to describe her homesteading adventure in Wyoming, Laura was joining a diverse group of women who wrote about living on the frontier. The structure and texture of Laura's manuscript marks it as the product of an observant woman committed to making sense of her time in the West.[22]

Almost Pioneers describes the processes involved in settling a homestead and building a community in the American West during the early twentieth century. The construction of shelter was primary, as

---

20 The University of Iowa Libraries, Iowa Women's Archives, "History & Mission of the Iowa Women's Archives," www.lib.uiowa.edu/iwa/history.html, accessed June 26, 2012; Michael Wheatcraft and Cathy Wheatcraft, conversation with author, March 19, 2008; Cathy Wheatcraft, telephone conversation with author, June 25, 2012.

21 Fry, *The Farm Press, Reform, and Rural Change, 1895–1920.*

22 A good introductory volume about women's autobiographical writing in the American West is *Women of the West*, edited by Cathy Luchetti and Carol Olwell (New York: Norton, 2001).

was the provision of a water supply. In addition, human connections were also immensely important. While their nearest neighbors lived miles away during the Smiths' first months in Wyoming, a number of families moved into the neighborhood during their second year. By the third year, a full-fledged neighborhood community had been established, enabling more permanent institutions to be built, including a school and the first approximation of a church. The book ends with that most American of community activities: an election.

There are two main parts of Smith's account, each of which takes up about half of the book. The first half of the volume, chapters 1 through 10, details Earle and Laura's first year in Wyoming. This half of the narrative provides extensive detail, describing how the Smiths moved to a claim shanty on a half-section of land miles away from civilization (represented by neighbors, town, city, and railroad) and built their first house. They settled in and figured out what was necessary to get by in their new surroundings, a process that some historians call "seasoning." Laura described it as a "complete and devastating break from the life we were accustomed to." The biggest obstacle they faced was lack of water. Every drop had to be hauled from a spring more than half a mile away, and Laura describes the many ways that they obtained and conserved water.

In this section Laura also compares the Casters, who were good neighbors, to the Bakers, who were bad neighbors. Ethel Caster's contributions to daily food production and her willingness to teach Laura how to bake bread show the Casters' willingness to give as well as take. This mutuality is contrasted with the selfishness and scheming of Mr. Baker. In addition, Luther and Ethel's evident love for each other and for their children enabled the children to accomplish what was necessary in a variety of circumstances. The Baker childrens' lack of skills can at least be partially blamed on the way that Mr. Baker treated them—and perhaps the way he had treated their mother. One wonders if Laura did not provide Mr. Baker's first name because she couldn't remember it, or because she just didn't want to identify him. She certainly remembered his children's names. On the other hand, the life of a single father raising adolescent children who were mourning the loss of their mother cannot have been easy. At any rate, the mutual help of husband, wife, and older children within the Caster family enabled them to help others. Laura's accounts show that the character of one's neighbors was as important to Westerners as one's shelter and access to water.

Boredom was another visitor during the first year. This makes one ponder why the Smiths hadn't taken more possessions along with them, especially if they knew they were going to be there for at least several months, and perhaps all winter. They were schoolteachers, not farmers, and they were not planning to do any farm work that year. Both of them had been accustomed to living in town, and now they were going to live in a small claim shanty. Why hadn't they at least brought some books to read?[23] I can think of two possibilities. The first was that they had absolutely no space left in their suitcases or trunks for books. But I believe it is more likely they just had no idea what living in Wyoming was going to be like. As a result, they just didn't think about bringing reading material. As Laura notes in chapter 4, they only gradually began to "realize how much we had always taken for granted as we saw how little we had and how hard it would be to get anything more." Many Americans moved west during the nineteenth and early twentieth centuries without knowing what to expect.

Chapter 10 describes the only time that either of the Smiths faced mortal danger during their sojourn in Wyoming. Earle's walk to Diamond through the snow to get to Iowa in time to teach could have resulted in disaster. Laura's narrative provides a simple and straightforward description of his efforts under the watchful eyes of the coyotes.

---

23 Rural people participated in the mainstream of American culture during the early twentieth century, and that included reading. See Fry, *The Farm Press, Reform, and Rural Change, 1895–1920*, chapter 3.

Instead of calamity, however, the story ends with only frostbitten feet. It becomes a good story to laugh about later—for instance, with Mr. Rainsford in chapter 15. Thus ended the Smiths' first year at the homestead.

The second half of the book describes the next two and a half years the Smiths spent on the homestead. Chapters 11 to 23 cover roughly the same number of pages as the first ten chapters. Laura's storytelling becomes less detailed and more episodic. In this section, she is especially interested in describing the development of a local community and the institutions that supported it. Other families moved close to the Smiths' homestead, including some good friends from Iowa, and the Smiths built their much more spacious second house closer to their neighbors. Laura describes the building of the area's first schoolhouse, a funeral for an infant, and the neighborhood's first Fourth of July celebration in 1914. Jessie Day and Laura tried to start a women's club with meetings every other week, but they found that their other neighbors were too busy to take the time to attend. Finally, the book tells of the first revival meetings and church services in the neighborhood, and the beginnings of political campaigning in the area.

Most likely, the religious community developed late for several reasons. First, the denominations that were favored by the characters in the story—the Presbyterian Church and the Christian Church (Disciples of Christ)—both required clergy to have a seminary education. Ministers were drawn from the upper middle class, who had the resources to fund years of theological training. Rural communities could rarely pay such a full-time minister; those who were willing to visit such a neighborhood were often not the most skilled pastors. It may also just be that the settlers were not very religious people. Only slightly more than a quarter of Wyoming residents at the time were members of a Christian church.[24]

---

24 "Figuring the percentage in each case on the population of the previous decennial census, Wyoming had 25.9 percent church members in 1906, 27.1 percent in 1916, 32 percent in 1926" (Larson, *History of Wyoming*, 446).

Earle and Laura's relationship to organized religion was mixed. In describing Earle's participation in the prairie funeral, Laura notes that "Earle was really not a very pious soul." His repeated use of "hell" in the foreword, his working all day on Sundays when building the second house (chapter 12), and his sharp criticism of Pastor Graham's foolishness in chapter 21 also suggest a lack of interest in Christianity. Jessie Day seems to have had the most desire for church services. In contrast to communities in the West which were built primarily on the cohesive force of deeply-held Christian beliefs,[25] Earle and Laura lived in a neighborhood of individuals thrown together by the land that the individuals had filed for. Christianity was most important to the community when residents needed to cope with the death of a family member, when they needed to bolster their courage in the face of physical challenges, and when they thought about passing their faith on to their children.

Thus, each partial year that the Smiths spent in Wyoming receives less treatment in the manuscript. While the first year takes up about half of the manuscript, the second year received less than a third, and the third year, less than that. One can imagine a few reasons for this decreasing level of description. Obviously, Laura's most vivid memories of her time in Wyoming were of that first year, when they were virtually alone on the prairie, miles away from clean water, and without much to do. Once a neighborhood community had formed, perhaps life became more routine, more like life in Iowa, and less interesting. My wife has suggested that the later years might have been harder for Laura—maybe because she now had a baby to take care of—and so she wrote less about them. Finally, Laura may have simply been

---

25 At about the same time, Jireh in east-central Wyoming was settled by Congregationalists, and Dutch Reformed Christians settled Manhattan, Montana, and several communities in southern Alberta. See Fama Hess Stoddard, "Jehovah Jireh (The Lord Will Provide)," *The Annals of Wyoming* 31(1), April 1959, 41–47; Donald Sinnema, ed., *The First Dutch Settlement in Alberta: Letters from the Pioneer Years, 1903–1914* (University of Calgary, 2005).

thinking about her audience, believing that her future readers would be most interested in her striking experiences during the first year. Her description of the family's final year in Wyoming only touches on community highlights.

One final observation is that Laura made creative decisions about how exactly to describe her experiences. Her choices concerning the framework of the book, the contrast between the Casters and the Bakers, and her description of the development of successive community institutions have already been noted. One final example is her presentation of two different ways of describing the natural landscape. For instance, at times she is lyrical and eloquent, as in this passage that opens the book:

> *There is a fascination about the vastness of the Western Plains, the rugged mountains, the uncertainty of the horizon, the crispness and clarity of the air and the brilliance of the sunshine that captures the imagination of anyone who comes to Wyoming and draws them back if they leave.*
>
> *In Wyoming's great spaces, winds blow over prairies and mountains, sending Russian thistles and tumbleweeds bounding for miles, piling winter snows in deep drifts or melting it like magic. Barbed-wire and buck fences stretch for miles; the atmosphere is so clear that mountains seem near, and stars shine so brilliantly they look to be within reach.*

On the other hand, the text also includes the more mundane and prosaic description of an empty and lonely landscape in the account of waiting for Earle at Diamond Station in chapter 2:

> *There was nothing in sight except the little station and one big, unpainted, rambling ranch house in the distance. . . .*
>
> *I looked out of each window in turn. There was nothing in sight except the rocky foothills and the box elders along the creek. Magpies*

*darted about in the trees, harshly calling to each other. I couldn't see a
trace of a man driving a wagon or a buggy.*

Both descriptions were clearly shaped for Laura's storytelling purpose.

Laura Gibson Smith approached her narrative of the family's time in Wyoming from a woman's point of view.[26] The book would be completely different if it had been written by Earle. However, both Laura and Earle were only visitors in the West. They never truly meant to settle in Wyoming.

Laura's identity as a visitor can be considered by placing *Almost Pioneers* in its regional context. The Smiths were temporary residents in southeastern Wyoming, in the area of Chugwater, and on the homestead itself. Southeastern Wyoming was a destination for dry-farming homesteaders mainly between 1907 and 1919. Homestead migration was encouraged by four developments: enforcement of anti-fencing laws, changes in federal homestead law, efforts on the part of Wyoming's government, and good weather.

In 1907 and 1908, the federal government attempted to put some teeth into laws against the fencing of the "public domain," which refers to land that still belonged to the United States. The federal government obtained control of this land via treaties with Native American groups that confined these groups to reservations during the late nineteenth century. Ranchers could run their cattle on the public domain, but they were not allowed to fence it. Nevertheless, large ranchers across the northern Great Plains had enclosed thousands of acres of federal land in violation of federal law. Early efforts at enforcement of anti-fencing laws came in the middle of the 1880s. A second round of enforcement

---

26 See the appendix for a consideration of *Almost Pioneers* in conversation with the works of Caroline Kirkland, Laura Ingalls Wilder, and Elinore Pruitt Stewart.

was undertaken between 1907 and 1909, during the Progressive Era's expansion of federal government authority. The Department of the Interior sent out federal marshals to investigate reports of the fencing of the public domain. Lawsuits against ranchers in violation of the law were filed in federal courts. If courts found against a rancher, he was fined and required to remove the fences; marshals cut the fences if ranchers did not comply with the decision. As a result, large areas of land in eastern Wyoming were opened for homesteading by the 1910s.[27]

Changes to federal homestead law also encouraged migration to southeastern Wyoming. The Homestead Act was originally passed in 1862. It stipulated that any individual or family could get 160 acres of land free from the United States if they lived on it for five years, nine months out of the year, and made improvements. A house had to be built, and at least forty acres had to be plowed and planted. By the early twentieth century, the homestead provision of federal land law had been amended multiple times. In 1909, the Enlarged Homestead Act raised the number of acres an individual or family could claim of semi-arid land to 320. More importantly, in 1912, the Three-Year Homestead Act lowered the number of years of residence from five to three, and lowered the number of months per year that one must reside on the homestead from nine to seven. The Smiths might have been less willing to spend forty-five months over five years to obtain land. As it happened, the number of farms in the state increased 75 percent between 1910 and 1935, and the amount of land in farms increased from 8.5 million acres to 28 million acres during that period.[28]

During the early 1910s, homestead migration was also encouraged by the activities of the Wyoming State Board of Immigration. It was created in 1911 by the state legislature and given a $40,000 budget to

---

27 Larson, *History of Wyoming*, 179–182; Phil Roberts, conversation with the author, May 22, 2008.

28 Hibbard, *A History of the Public Land Policies*, 393–396; Brown, *Wyoming: A Geography*, 72.

draw homesteaders. During its two years of operation, it mailed out over 300,000 letters and pieces of literature. The Board encouraged emigrants to come from Nebraska, South Dakota, Colorado, Kansas, and Iowa. Wyoming's commissioner of immigration, Roy W. Schenk, used state money to bring correspondents from Eastern newspapers to Cheyenne. He also took an exhibit titled "Wyoming, The Land of Great Reward" to Chicago, Pittsburgh, and New York City, and delivered lectures encouraging farmers to come to Wyoming. The Wyoming legislature defunded the Immigration Board in 1913, due to lack of results. Nonetheless, it may be that the Smiths and their friends and neighbors from Iowa found out about homesteading opportunities because of the efforts of this board.[29]

Finally, immigration to southeastern Wyoming was promoted by good weather during the 1900s and 1910s. It appears that the years that the Smiths homesteaded were unusually wet years for the entire region. The mean precipitation for Chugwater during the twentieth century was about sixteen inches.[30] Normally twenty inches of rainfall is necessary for growing crops such as the wheat grown by the Smiths. Between 1910 and 1915, it appears that on a regular basis there was sufficient rainfall for the growing of wheat using dry-farming methods. Thus, the Smiths may have homesteaded during the best possible time. Precipitation was decreasing during the late 1910s, and drought hit southeastern Wyoming in 1919. This coincided with the post–World War I decrease in food prices caused by European countries consistently growing their own crops again. As a result, dry-farming agriculture in Wyoming was devastated during the 1920s and 1930s.

---

29 Larson, *History of Wyoming*, 359–365; Western, *Pushed Off the Mountain, Sold Down the River*, 34–40.

30 NOAA / National Weather Service preliminary data; Barbara Mayes Boustead, NOAA, e-mail message to author, September 23, 2010.

Wet weather did not return again until the late 1930s, and good prices not until World War II.[31]

The town of Chugwater itself experienced dramatic growth during the middle of the 1910s. One can trace this growth in the pages of the *Wyoming State Business Directory* during the decade. In the 1912–13 edition of the *Directory*, Chugwater was described as a "Station on the Colorado and Southern Railroad, in Laramie County, 72 miles north of Cheyenne. Stock raising the leading industry. Population 50."[32] There were five businesses listed: a blacksmith, a realtor, the trading company, the telephone company, and the Swan Land and Cattle Company. In the 1914 edition, the population was listed as 150. Fifteen businesses were described, including a hardware store, a plumber, a barber, two carpenters, and the Swan Mercantile Company. According to an article in the *Wyoming Semi-Weekly Tribune* in May of 1914, Chugwater was hoping to capitalize on increased agricultural production and settlement, and was preparing to auction off 450 town-site lots.[33] Three years later, the population had increased to 300, and there are forty-nine listings in the *Business Directory*. The farmers' cooperative elevator and store, the *Chugwater Record* newspaper, two hotels, one bank, and the Baptist and Episcopal churches both make their appearance in this volume. However, during the rest of the 1910s, the population and number of establishments remained relatively the same.[34]

---

31 Duane A. Smith, *Rocky Mountain West: Colorado, Wyoming, and Montana, 1859–1915* (Albuquerque: University of New Mexico, 1992), 223; *Wyoming Voices* (Cheyenne: Wyoming Public Television, 2004) Part II, "A New Century, 1892–1942," video recording; Larson, *History of Wyoming*, 414–418.

32 *Wyoming State Business Directory, 1912–1913* (Denver: Gazetteer, 1912), 203.

33 *Wyoming State Business Directory, 1914* (Denver: Gazetteer, 1914), 103; "Chugwater Town Site Lots to be Sold on May 26th: New Town, Sixty Miles North of Cheyenne, Is Situated in Best Part of Platte County's Great Agricultural District," *Wyoming Semi-Weekly Tribune*, May 8, 1914.

34 *Wyoming State Business Directory, 1917*, 230–232; *Wyoming State Business Directory, 1918*, 219–221; *Wyoming State Business Directory, 1919*, 206–208; *Wyoming State Business Directory, 1920*, 186–188; all were published in Denver by the Gazetteer Publishing Company.

The *Business Directory* also provided listings for Diamond. Unlike Chugwater's, Diamond's descriptions display little change over the decade. In 1912–13 the entire entry was: "Station on the Colorado and Southern Railroad and post office in Laramie County, 61 miles north of Cheyenne. Stock raising the leading industry. Population 10."[35] This record remained the same until 1916, when the listing included the postmaster, W. R. Day (most likely the Dr. Day of our story), and the "Robinson Bros, fuel and feed, groceries," most likely the Uncle Billy Robinson of chapter 16 and the Robinson School mentioned in chapters 12, 14, and 23. The next year's directory added "Gillaspie, Elvy, general merchandise." All directories for the decade listed the population as ten. Diamond had a post office from 1894 to 1940.[36]

During the 1900s and 1910s, in Wyoming newspapers, inhabitants of the Smiths' neighborhood were either described as being from Diamond or from Chugwater. By the middle of the twentieth century, however, the neighborhood inhabited by the Smiths, Casters, and others had become included as part of a larger neighborhood known as the Little Bear Community. Today it stretches southeast toward County Road 238. Exit 39 on Interstate 25 is labeled "Little Bear Community." There was a US post office for Little Bear close to that location from 1877 to 1955.[37]

Census records for Chugwater are available since 1920. In fact, the population in 1920 was higher than any recorded figure ever since. Census figures are given in table 1. While population fluctuated between about 240 and 280 from 1930 to 1960, Chugwater lost

---

35 *Wyoming State Business Directory, 1912–1913*, 225.

36 *Wyoming State Business Directory, 1916* (Denver: Gazetteer, 1916), 226; *Wyoming State Business Directory, 1917*, 254; *Wyoming State Business Directory, 1918*, 241; *Wyoming State Business Directory, 1920*, 241. John S. Gallagher and Alan H. Patera, Wyoming Post Offices: 1850–1950 (Burtonsville, MD: The Depot, 1980), 104.

37 "Little Changes at Little Bear," *Wyoming Tribune-Eagle*, March 17, 1998; Gallagher and Patera, Wyoming Post Offices: 1850–1950, 80.

Table 1. Population of Chugwater, Wyoming

1890	53
1900	49
1910	49
1920	315
1930	286
1940	245
1950	283
1960	287
1970	187
1980	282
1990	192
2000	244
2010	212

Sources: Riley Moffat, *Population History of Western US Cities and Towns, 1850–1990* (Lanham, Maryland: Scarecrow, 1996), 339; US Census, "Wyoming—Place, Population, Housing Units, Area, and Density: 2000," available at http://census.gov (accessed June 22, 2010); US Census, "2010 Census Interactive Population Search, WY—Chugwater—Town," available at http://census.gov (accessed June 26, 2012).

a third of its residents during the 1960s. This was most likely due to the decline of local ranching during these years and the town being bypassed by Interstate 25 in 1969. There were fewer opportunities in agriculture to make a living that compared with the standard of living possible working in urban areas, inside or outside the state. Across the state, the number of farms, number of acres in farms, and number of farm workers all decreased by more than 50 percent between 1935 and 1969. Some families moved into the area with the construction of a major power plant in Wheatland in the early 1970s. Periodic increases and decreases have continued since 1980.[38]

The Smiths went to Wyoming and homesteaded with no serious intention of staying there. They hoped to obtain land they could lease out and use the money to underwrite other pursuits. How many others pursued land in the West for reasons other than actual settlement? This is difficult for historians to answer definitively. "Speculators" have always played a role in Western land settlement. During the early 1800s, wealthy Americans in the old Southwest or Midwest claimed government land and waited for it to improve in price in order to sell it. In the middle of the century, railroads were granted millions of acres of land to get the transcontinental railroad and other railroads built. In Wyoming in the late 1800s, some cowboys homesteaded land in order to sell it to their ranch employers, either voluntarily or under duress.[39] As far as percentages of those who persisted and those who did not, historians who studied the Midwest in the early 1800s found that from one decennial census to the next, about 30 percent of residents of an area persisted. Those who left may have done so because their farms failed and they moved back east, because they decided to sell out and move west, or for other, more personal reasons. Of those mentioned in this book, it appears that fairly quickly after proving up, the Smiths and Days moved back to Iowa. Members of the Duvall, Long, Gillaspie, Cline, and Derby families stayed. However, it is impossible to know exactly why individual families made the decisions that they

38 Brown, *Wyoming: A Geography*, 75–77; *Wyoming Voices* (Cheyenne: Wyoming Public Television, 2004) Part III, "Powder River Let 'er Buck, video recording; Rod Lockman, *Chugwater Comprehensive Plan* (Boulder: Western Interstate Commission for Higher Education, 1976), 2–3; Andy Field and Alex Nitzman, "Interstate 25" at www.aaroads.com/west/i-025_wy.html, accessed May 15, 2012.

39 Stephen Aron, "Pioneers and Profiteers: Land Speculation and the Homestead Ethic in Frontier Kentucky," *Western Historical Quarterly* 23 (1992): 179–198; Allan Bogue, *From Prairie to Corn Belt: Farming on the Illinois and Iowa Prairies in the Nineteenth Century* (University of Chicago, 1963), chapter 2; Larson, *History of Wyoming*, 173–178.

did. Laura and Earle were not the only homesteaders in southeastern Wyoming who were ultimately only visitors.[40]

Of all of Luther and Mary Ethel Caster's large family—they eventually had seven children: Osa, Cecil, Wayne, Clyde, James, Wrex [*sic*], and Luther—only Clyde Caster remained in the neighborhood. As is noted in the epilogue, Luther and Ethel moved back to Moravia, Iowa; their youngest son Luther went with them. Osa married a local homesteader and moved to Colorado; Cecil and Wayne also moved to Colorado. James moved to Oregon late in his life, and Wrex worked in mines in Laramie County and retired to Cheyenne. Clyde became a rancher and leased the land of a number of the homesteaders mentioned in this book. In 1931, he married ENeva [*sic*] Duvall, a daughter of Roy Duvall. In 1967, Laura and Earle sold the homestead land to Clyde and ENeva. For years Clyde used the house the Smiths had built for storage of animal feed. Sometime during the 1980s, he and his family spent significant time improving the condition of the building. They put up sheetrock walls and ceilings in the upstairs, stuccoed the exterior, and replaced the roof. As a result, the house still stands.[41]

On a bright and clear morning in late spring of 2008, I drove the forty-five miles north on Interstate 25 from Cheyenne to Chugwater. There I met Dean and Ruth Vaughn at Horton's Corner, the gas station right off of the interstate, and we drove south in their minivan on county roads. Ruth is Clyde Caster's daughter. After driving parallel to

40 John Mack Faragher, *Sugar Creek: Life on the Illinois Prairie* (New Haven: Yale, 1986), 50–52, 249n; Mildred Thorne, "Population Study of an Iowa County in 1850," *Iowa Journal of History* 57(1959): 305–350; James C. Malin, "The Turnover of Farm Population in Kansas," *Kansas Historical Quarterly* 4 (1935): 339–372; Tract records, Laramie County Clerk's Office, Cheyenne, Wyoming.

41 Ruth Vaughn, Clyde Caster Jr., and Frances Caster, conversations with author, Laramie County, Wyoming, May 23, 2008, June 21, 2012; Warranty Deed, November 21, 1967, Laramie County Clerk's Office, Cheyenne, Wyoming.

The rock house, 2008. Electric lines were run to the house during the 1980s.
AUTHOR'S COLLECTION

the interstate for about seven miles, we entered Laramie County and turned west. All of the county roads from Chugwater to the site of the Smiths' homestead are paved. When I remarked on this, the Vaughns explained that there are nuclear missile silos on these roads, and therefore the United States government paid for the roads to be paved to the silos during the Cold War. After the last silo on a road, the pavement stops and the road becomes gravel—or gravel and mud, depending on how much rain there has been.[42]

---

42 For a brief explanation of Wyoming's role in the Cold War, see Brown, *Wyoming: A Geography*, 2–4. Most of these silos have since been decommissioned (Ruth Vaughn, Clyde Caster Jr., and Frances Caster, conversations with author, Laramie County, Wyoming, May 23, 2008, June 21, 2012).

When turning the corner from County Road 242 onto County Road 116, one can see the Smiths' house on the top of a ridge. At this corner, one passes the current home of Clyde Caster Jr. and his wife Frances on the right. Then, after another half-mile, one can pull off the road to the left and drive up to the house itself. As one stands on the ridge and looks out at the horizon, many things indicate that nearly a hundred years have passed since Earle and Laura Smith built this house. High-voltage power lines run from the horizon northeast to southeast. Missile silos dot the landscape, sitting low behind chain-link fences. The Casters' fifteen-year-old house is visible to the north-west. Still, one can imagine what the landscape must have looked like to two young Iowans in the early years of the twentieth century. The sky is enormous, the wind blows constantly, and the undulating plains spread out in all directions.

As Laura explained, the house itself is split-entry; upon entering the side door, one is confronted by two twenty-inch-wide staircases—one on the right going up, and one on the left going down. Excluding the side entrance area, the house is twenty feet long by ten feet wide. One can see the chimney and where the stove must have stood down-stairs, and the heater upstairs. The steps, banister, and floor upstairs are the original wood. The walls downstairs are the original concrete and rock. The stone porch still stands, although the roof no longer extends out over it.

It must have been a comfortable home for the two young adults, counting their days until they could prove up on their claim. It is also incredibly small by today's standards. Measuring off ten by twenty feet of one's own living room can give one an idea of how much space the Smiths had to move around in, even if there were two stories. In addi-tion, for long periods of time they shared the house with a boarder. The house feels extremely cramped to a twenty-first-century Ameri-can. The stairs are narrow and the ceilings are low. Nonetheless, the

One view from the rock house, 2008. AUTHOR'S COLLECTION

edifice blocks the Wyoming wind and the windows allow one to look over the grasslands in all directions.

I visited the homestead again four years later. This time, Clyde Caster also took me to Little Bear Cemetery to visit the grave of Nancy Black, the infant whose funeral is described in chapter 13. This was a major undertaking, because rains had washed out the dirt roads that led to the site. This meant that getting there involved negotiating a meandering course through a number of fields. We took Clyde's 1990 pickup truck. The trails we drove were used by ranchers and cattle, but we bumped up and down over rocks, dips, and ruts. It was windy and dry, and the pickup did not have air conditioning. I observed that perhaps this trip roughly approximated the kind of trips that Laura and Earle took across the plains in a wagon or the top buggy. Clyde assured me that his mother had told him stories about riding in a wagon, and it was much worse. It took about forty-five minutes to make the five-mile trip.

Once at the cemetery, there was not a house in sight. Signs of twenty-first-century civilization were still visible, including high-line electrical wires in the west, Interstate 25 in the distance to the east, and lower electrical wires in all directions. But one could feel the solitude. Here I stood, as Laura described it, near that "lonely bare hillside grave with the moaning wind blowing over the prairie." I was raised on a hundred-acre farm in western Pennsylvania, but here thousands of treeless acres extended to the horizon. I felt incredibly small and isolated.

Undoubtedly, on these two occasions, I was just a visitor to Wyoming. It was moving to visit these places where Laura and Earle had lived and walked. It felt like I had a real connection to them. However, the experience of visiting a historic location can also be deceiving. In fact, much of what I saw did not exist in the past. Natural growth of foliage, changes to landforms over time, and changes due to human occupation all guarantee that the place I was looking at was not what the Smiths saw. Despite this, I could imagine what it was like for two Iowans and their infant son, visitors to Wyoming nearly one hundred years ago. The landscape I observed was briefly the home of three Americans.

Laura and Earle's identity as Americans points to a final context for considering *Almost Pioneers*. There are two ways to locate the Smiths' homesteading adventure in the American national experience. One is as an example of the pursuit of opportunity in the face of hardships.

It is a story of willingness to accept less in order to have more in the future. The other is as a cautionary tale about the costs of both individualism and the quest for prosperity.

The first way to fit *Almost Pioneers* into American history is optimistic. The book talks about the hardships that the Smith family faced, like many before them in other parts of the West. They struggled with distance from neighbors, lack of water, and fear of rattlesnakes. The Smiths endured these hardships to better their economic position, illustrating an American trait: willingness to go backward in order to go forward. It may be that this trait is a key to understanding how ordinary Americans have made the United States the most prosperous and free country in the world. The Smiths' story provides a view of this process in the life of one family.[43]

This trait was at the center of Frederick Jackson Turner's famous essay, "The Significance of the Frontier in American History." Turner argued that the existence of free land emancipated Americans from previous institutions and lowered the standards of civilization, making Americans more nationalistic, more democratic, and more individualistic.[44] In the Smiths' case, freedom from institutions, lowered standards, and individualism appear to be true. Nevertheless, it is evident that the Smiths and their neighbors attempted to re-create those community institutions quickly. More importantly, Laura and Earle returned east to reap the benefits of the "free land" they had received from the government.

In fact, the Smiths' story is more accurately described by historian David Potter in *People of Plenty*, published in 1954. For Potter, it was not the frontier but the general existence of economic abundance that characterizes American society and formed American character. (He

---

43 This trait is insightfully described by *New York Times* columnist David Brooks in *On Paradise Drive: How We Live Now (And Always Have) In the Future Tense* (New York: Simon and Schuster, 2004), esp. chapter 9.

44 Frederick Jackson Turner, "The Significance of the Frontier in American History," in *The Frontier in American History* (New York: Henry Holt, 1920, first published 1893), 19–36.

observed, as others have, that Turner never really settled on whether the frontier was a place, a condition, or a process.) Potter wrote:

> *The frontier, with its necessity for some reduction of living standards, could attract people from settled areas so long as the existing standards in those areas did not exceed a certain maximum (people would accept a certain unfavorable differential in their current standards for the sake of potential gain). But when existing city standards exceeded this maximum, when the differential became too great, people would no longer accept it even for all the future rewards that the frontier might promise. . . . In short, the frontier ceased to operate as a major force in American history not when it disappeared . . . but when the primary means of access to abundance passed from the frontier to other focuses in American life.*[45]

This appears to fit the Smiths' calculations well. They were willing to leave the comforts of small-town Iowa at the turn of the twentieth century for a short time, but not for the rest of their lives.

It was in the early twentieth century that land availability stopped being one of the primary ways of getting ahead in the United States. There were many Western farmers that failed in the late-nineteenth- and early-twentieth-century West. Many failures on the Plains contributed to the rise of the Populist Party in the 1890s. In the 1930s, federal New Deal programs attempted to assist Western farmers who were failing due to drought and low prices.[46] During these two eras, and the years between them, thousands of Western farmers simply pulled up stakes and moved back east. Americans—especially Westerners—are

---

45   David M. Potter, *People of Plenty: Economic Abundance and the American Character* (University of Chicago, 1958), 159–160.

46   Robert C. McMath Jr., *American Populism: A Social History, 1877–1898* (New York: Hill and Wang, 1993), 19–50; David M. Kennedy, *Freedom from Fear: The American People in Depression and War, 1929–1945* (New York: Oxford, 1999), 190–202.

not used to talking about failure. Myths that have grown up around the American West are predicated on success. As one historian observed, "That old West, that land of opportunity, would not die. Since the days of Jamestown and Plymouth, the West had beckoned, a land in which a new start could be made, a fortune won. Though many chose to ignore the fact, it could also be the place where one could fail and the dream turn to ashes. . . . There was a dark side to the American dream."[47]

The Smiths were not failures; it appears that they had always planned to move back to Iowa. However, many other homesteaders were driven out of the arid Western plains, including southwestern Wyoming, in the late 1910s.[48] Earle and Laura realized that the way to fulfill their dreams was not to farm free land in the West, but to pursue further education. They succeeded in obtaining both land and Earle's law degree, and thus realized the American dream of self-reliance and economic security.

The Smiths' identity as Americans can also illuminate the darker side of the American experience. First, the Smiths' access to their 320-acre homestead was made possible not only by the federal government's enforcement of anti-fencing laws, but also by their extinguishing of Native American title to the land. Few Native American groups ever made Wyoming their permanent home, but a handful of groups lived there temporarily as they hunted buffalo. During the 1860s and 1870s, the Shoshone and Arapaho were restricted to the Wind River Reservation in the central portion of Wyoming Territory. During the 1880s and 1890s, the Dakota were confined to the Pine Ridge and Rosebud reservations, in what would eventually become South Dakota. Thus, the federal government cleared the way for white American ranchers and homesteaders to claim and take possession of land that had been used by others for centuries. I am not arguing that Laura and Earle were

---

47   Smith, *Rocky Mountain West: Colorado, Wyoming, and Montana, 1859–1915*, 122.

48   Larson, *History of Wyoming*, 386–411. See also Paula M. Nelson, *After the West Was Won: Homesteaders and Town-Builders in Western South Dakota, 1900–1917* (Iowa City: University of Iowa, 1986), 120–141.

responsible for the Native American wars, broken treaties, and other actions of the federal government, but we should remember that history does have its winners and losers. Opportunity that is granted to one group sometimes comes at the expense of another.[49]

In addition, one might consider the costs of the Smiths' undertaking. Launching out into the unknown involves an individualism that values opportunity, autonomy, and prosperity over community, responsibility, and stability. Laura's manuscript describes the building of the neighborhood community in Wyoming and how it provided support when Earle left her alone with her infant son to teach in Iowa. However, once they had proved up on the land, the Smiths left that community to seek opportunity elsewhere. That search led them to the Philippines, to Iowa, to Florida, and then back to Iowa. By the 1950s, they had become financially independent, mobile, and in control of their lives; however, perhaps they missed out on the deeper joys made possible by a long-term commitment to one place and one community. In the early nineteenth century, Alexis de Tocqueville, the keen observer and analyst of American society, worried that American ways of life might create an unhealthy individualism that would degenerate into mere selfishness. During the last half-century, the poems, essays, and novels of Wendell Berry have meditated in a variety of ways on this loss of community and what it means for modern life.[50]

There were also more tangible costs to the Smiths' activities. The Homestead Act was designed to encourage settlement, yet the Smiths did not go there to settle; they went to obtain property as an investment. Once they had obtained title to the land, they leased it. In effect, they were speculators who became absentee landlords. While owning land

---

49 Larson, *History of Wyoming*, 33–34, 106–107; White, *"It's Your Misfortune and None of My Own,"* chapter 2.

50 Alexis de Tocqueville, *Democracy in America,* trans. and ed. Harvey C. Mansfield and Delba Winthrop (University of Chicago, 2000), 482–488, 500–503. A good brief introduction to Berry's work is J. Matthew Bonzo and Michael R. Stevens, *Wendell Berry and the Cultivation of Life: A Reader's Guide* (Grand Rapids, MI: Brazos, 2008).

in Wyoming made it possible for Earle to finish law school and finance other life pursuits, as long as they owned the land, the Smiths were taking money out of the local economy. They continued to do this for fifty years.

So, which is it? Were the Smiths quintessential Americans, launching out into the unknown to better their position financially, willing to go backwards for a short period of time in order to make a better future for themselves and their son, and helping to build the prosperous and free nation that we enjoy today? Or were the Smiths quintessential Americans, only looking out for their own interests without regard for those who had come before them, or the needs of their local community? Whether one prefers the first narrative of American history or the second may primarily depend on where one's views fall on the political spectrum. The political Right in the early twenty-first century tends to see the history of the United States as the story of ever-expanding freedom and opportunity for all Americans. The political Left prefers to trace the oppression of minorities, workers, and women in US history, emphasizing the missed opportunities in American history for real equality and community.[51]

---

51 For good examples of the two competing views of American history, see Larry Schweikart and Michael Allen, *A Patriot's History of the United States* (New York: Penguin, 2004) and Howard Zinn, *A People's History of the United States* (New York: HarperCollins, 1980). See also the interaction of two different views of the West applied to central Wyoming in Tom Rea's *Devil's Gate: Owning the Land, Owning the Story* (Norman: University of Oklahoma, 2006). I believe that the position of historic Christianity provides a way beyond the extremes of these two positions. According to this view, the Bible teaches that God created humans in His image and to bring Him glory, and that He is involved in human history, working out His purposes. As a result, the improvement of individuals' lives in terms of freedom, opportunity, and prosperity are the result of humans' God-given creative abilities and His grace. However, all humans are also fallen, twisted, and selfish. As a result, even our greatest accomplishments are tainted by brokenness. This perspective allows one to rejoice with the Smiths as they complete the requirements to obtain the land that will underwrite future successes even as one considers the possible costs of their actions for others. See George M. Marsden, "A Christian Perspective for the Teaching of History" in George Marsden and Frank Roberts, eds., *A Christian View of History?* (Grand Rapids, MI: Eerdmans, 1975), 31–49, and John J. Fry, "History as a Tutor to Lead us to Christ: Outrageous Idea or Modest Proposal," unpublished manuscript presented at the 2004 Conference on Faith and History Biennial Meeting, Holland, Michigan, October 15, 2004.

There is truth in both characterizations of American history and both understandings of the Smiths' actions. However, it is unfair to Laura and Earle to too heavily weigh down their life stories with either the commendations of the Right or the condemnations of the Left. While one can view their biography through different lenses influenced by modern-day concerns, one should also respect the Smiths' story as *their* story. Their lives may merely be seen as two of the millions of individual threads that make up the tapestry of American history. Their story can be enjoyed for what it is.

Earle and Laura Smith were Iowans. Sojourns in Wyoming and the Philippine Islands punctuated their early marriage. They lived in Florida near the end of Laura's life, but Earle moved back to Iowa permanently after her death. Laura was also a woman who wrote about the American West. She described the landscape of the West, her adjustment to Western life, and the community in which they lived in the early twentieth century, shaping her narrative and description to her purposes and audience. Laura and Earle were visitors in Wyoming, taking advantage of United States government policy to better their economic position. Finally, the Smiths were Americans, willing to go backward in order to slingshot forward. They gave up the comforts of life for a while so that they could have a better life when they resettled in Iowa. The Smiths experienced great geographic mobility, and they had an adventure in the West, but they ultimately left Wyoming to realize the American dream.

APPENDIX:

LAURA GIBSON SMITH IN CONVERSATION WITH OTHER WESTERN WOMEN WRITERS
by John J. Fry

ONE WAY OF CONSIDERING LAURA GIBSON SMITH AS A WOMAN WHO wrote about the American West is to analyze the structure, texture, and content of *Almost Pioneers*. My analysis is presented as one portion of the afterword. This appendix will present a second way of appraising Smith as a Western woman writer: drawing comparisons between her work and that of three other women who wrote about the West during the nineteenth and early twentieth centuries: Caroline Kirkland, Laura Ingalls Wilder, and Elinore Pruitt Stewart.

Caroline Kirkland was born in New York City in 1801, the first of eleven children. She met her future husband, William Kirkland, in western New York, and they were married in 1828. Seven years later the family moved to Detroit, and in 1837 they moved sixty miles west of the town to the frontier village of Pinckney, Michigan. Like the Smiths, both of the Kirklands taught school, William at Hamilton College in Clinton, New York, and Caroline as head of a women's seminary in Detroit. His pursuit of opportunity in the country did not reward them financially, but she was able to write a book about her experiences during the first couple of years. *A New Home, Who'll Follow? or Glimpses of Western Life*, a satirical look at rural life, was published in 1839.[1] Kirkland adopted the fictional name of Mary Clavers,

---

[1] The book has been republished with a scholarly introduction and bibliography: Caroline M. Kirkland, *A New Home, Who'll Follow? or Glimpses of Western Life* (New Brunswick, NJ: Rutgers University, 1990).

renamed the village they lived in Montacute, and added some fictional accounts to her descriptions. However, because her proclaimed purpose was to provide a "detailed account of our experiences" and a "veracious history of actual occurrences," scholars have taken most of the accounts in the book as representing actual events.[2]

The Kirklands' experiences were similar to the Smiths'. Both families underwent "seasoning" in accommodations during their first year that were less than satisfactory: the Smiths in a dugout, the Kirklands in a log cabin. After about a year, the Kirklands were able to move into a frame house which was larger and much more convenient. In addition, both women had to adjust to being far from home and out of touch with family. The Smiths received mail only when Earle or a neighbor rode to Diamond; Kirkland speaks glowingly of when weekly mail service was established in their community. Caroline and Laura also both describe the development of neighborhood institutions including a school, religious services, and politics.[3]

However, there are also significant divergences in how the two women described their experiences. Moving to the West during the early nineteenth century was different than moving there during the early twentieth. Frontier Michigan was not frontier Wyoming. The Kirklands had multiple neighbors within walking distance when they moved to Pinckney; the Smiths had to have a horse to reach neighbors during their first year in Wyoming. Much of Kirkland's book depicts her adjustment to the lack of genteel and civilized surroundings. It presents a description of rural Michigan from the point of view of a well-bred, well-educated, and well-heeled New Yorker. Kirkland laments the lack of availability of servants, the presence of dirt, and the absence of refined home accoutrements.[4] Smith, on the other hand,

---

2   Kirkland, 3; Kolodny, *The Land Before Her*, 133–135.

3   Kirkland, 145, 177–178.

4   Kirkland, 1–49.

like most small-town Iowans during the early twentieth century, had few pretensions to gentility. Comments about her clothes in the initial chapters suggest that she accepted fairly quickly that she would not be able to dress or act the same way in Wyoming as she had previously. Her only real concerns about gentility involve her ability to say and do the right thing when visiting wealthy Mr. Rainsford in chapter 15. Smith did desire a certain amount of comfort; she preferred riding in a buggy to horseback, and she did convince her husband to build a second, more-comfortable house closer to neighbors. However, this was vastly different from the pursuit of refinement and civilization described in Kirkland's book.

It is also fascinating to compare the two authors' descriptions of the local women's club, church, and politics. In contrast to Smith's failed club, Kirkland joyfully describes the foibles of the local Female Benevolent Society, whose meetings were rocked by gossip, accusations, and backbiting. Again, however, because Pinckney women lived much closer to one another, such an institution was much easier to organize than in a southeastern Wyoming neighborhood. Kirkland also seems to have somewhat more genuine interest in Christianity than Smith, although she also doesn't address the church until late in her book (chapter 33 out of 47). Kirkland is even more blunt in describing most traveling preachers as incompetent. Like Smith, she notes the competition between denominations in American Christianity.[5] Finally, whereas the centerpiece of Smith's account of politics is an election, Kirkland's description of politics is mainly confined to discussing the local justice of the peace and the litigious nature of rural Midwesterners.[6]

---

5   Kirkland, 127–139.

6   Kirkland, 170–177. These were the same years that Abraham Lincoln was making his fortune as a lawyer, especially in the rural counties of central Illinois; see Brian Dirck, *Lincoln the Lawyer* (Urbana: University of Illinois, 2009).

Still, Kirkland's description of the happiest Westerners rings true when applied to the Smiths:

> *[Many are] young married people just beginning the world; simple in their habits, moderate in their aspirations, and hoarding a little of old-fashioned romance, unconsciously enough, in the secret nooks of their rustic hearts. . . . They have youth, and health, and love and hope, occupation and amusement, and when you have added "meat, clothes, and fire," what more has England's fair young queen? These people are contented, of course.*[7]

How better to describe Laura and Earle in the third year of their sojourn, perched in their house on the ridge overlooking the treeless grasslands? Their ample dinner is over, baby Bert is in his cradle, and Earle reads from *The Saturday Evening Post* as Laura prepares the bread sponge for the subsequent day. There is also a final similarity between the Smiths and the Kirklands. The latter—partially because of complaints from their neighbors about the frankness of descriptions in *A New Home,* and partially because of financial challenges—moved back east to New York City in 1843.[8]

Laura Ingalls Wilder is another example of a Western woman writer during the early twentieth century. Like Smith (and unlike Kirkland, who wrote while living in Pinckney), Wilder wrote about her experiences some time after they happened. Laura Ingalls was born in the "Big Woods" of Wisconsin in 1867. Her family moved to Kansas in 1869, then back to Wisconsin two years later. By 1879, when Laura was twelve, the family had also lived in Minnesota and briefly in Iowa. That year, the family moved into Dakota Territory. Her father, Charles Ingalls, successfully homesteaded a 160-acre farm outside of

---

7   Kirkland, 145–146.

8   Kolodny, 145.

the new town of DeSmet. Laura married Almanzo Wilder in 1885. However, the young couple failed to prove up on their homestead due to drought, sickness, and personal tragedy. The early twentieth century found the Wilder family living on a farm in the Ozarks outside of Mansfield, Missouri.[9] Laura began writing her autobiography in the late 1920s, hoping to get a magazine to publish it in serial form. While no magazines were interested, Harper and Brothers published a book of her father's stories in 1932 as *Little House in the Big Woods*. During the next eleven years, the other seven *Little House* books were published.[10]

There are several similarities between *Almost Pioneers* and the *Little House* books. First, like Kirkland, both authors pay great attention to the "seasoning" process of moving to a new place and settling in. In addition, both women provide descriptions of the houses that they lived in and how they were built, although Wilder's descriptions are much more detailed. For instance, Wilder's narrative of the construction of their log cabin in Kansas in *Little House on the Prairie* spans multiple chapters. There are also painstaking descriptions of other houses in later volumes.[11] Wilder's books also first describe the seasoning process and then successive stages of community building. This pattern occurs repeatedly for the various locations the family lived

---

9   The most reliable biographies of Laura Ingalls Wilder are William Anderson, *Laura Ingalls Wilder: A Biography* (New York: HarperCollins, 1992), written for young readers; John E. Miller, *Becoming Laura Ingalls Wilder: The Woman Behind the Legend* (Columbia: University of Missouri, 1998), a full-scale scholarly biography and the best to date; and Pamela Smith Hill, *Laura Ingalls Wilder: A Writer's Life* (Pierre: South Dakota State Historical Society, 2007).

10   The *Little House* books are *Little House in the Big Woods* (1932), *Farmer Boy* (1933), *Little House on the Prairie* (1935), *On the Banks of Plum Creek* (1937), *By the Shores of Silver Lake* (1939), *The Long Winter* (1940), *Little Town on the Prairie* (1941), and *These Happy Golden Years* (1943). All were published in New York by Harper and Brothers, and all were edited by Laura's daughter Rose. *Farmer Boy* describes Almanzo's boyhood in upstate New York, not Laura's life. Subsequent notes give page numbers from the revised edition of all the books published by Harper in 1953.

11   *Little House on the Prairie,* 52–70, 99–106, 120–131; *On the Banks of Plum Creek,* 10–17, 109–117; *By the Shores of Silver Lake,* 141–150, 247–263.

in during Wilder's childhood. Her books describe the development of the family's interactions with neighborhood, school, church, and, eventually, politics.

Another point of similarity between Wilder and Smith is the role of Christianity in the two women's lives. As the church is one of the later community institutions introduced in Smith's book, the church does not appear in the narrative of Wilder's life until about halfway through the third volume, *On the Banks of Plum Creek*. Organized religion's appearance comes after descriptions of the neighborhood community, the one-room schoolhouse, and parties with schoolmates. Laura's father announces one Saturday night that they will be going to church the next day, and Laura as narrator notes that "Laura and Mary had never seen a church."[12]

Wilder's treatment of the church in the later *Little House* books is also somewhat detached, although she and her family did have more connections to the church than the Smiths did. The Wilders attended church services weekly whenever possible, and they were active in the social opportunities provided by the church, such as Christmas parties and ladies aid sociables. However, Laura's dislike of the pastor of the Congregational church in DeSmet means that she makes comments about his "long stupid sermons." She also relates that, during the worship service, she was required by her father to remember the Bible passage that was read, but "then she need not listen any more."[13] Both women's books clearly depict an ambivalent relationship to organized Christianity.

Finally, both Wilder and Smith position themselves as young women learning from those who were older and more experienced. Ma Ingalls, the center of the domestic universe in the *Little House* books, is never at a loss when it involves cooking or other domestic

---

12 *On the Banks of Plum Creek*, 178.

13 *These Happy Golden Years*, 42. *Becoming Laura Ingalls Wilder*, 102–105, 131.

duties. She quietly, carefully, and competently teaches Laura and other young women how to make bread. In addition, a major theme in the later volumes is how Ma prepares Laura for marriage.[14] Laura Smith likewise situates herself as a novice at navigating life in the West. She never quite masters baking bread, and she is at a loss when it comes to many other domestic duties. To a great extent, Ethel Caster and Mrs. Day function as mothers for Smith during her stay in Wyoming. In fact, a number of the other women in the book are depicted as taking a matter-of-fact approach to life and ultimately being in control of themselves and their surroundings, including her mother (chapter 17), Mrs. Day when her husband is injured (chapter 18), and Mrs. Gillaspie's management while her husband was gone (chapter 20).

However, there are also differences between Wilder and Smith's descriptions. For instance, Ma Ingalls and her entire family seem to display some of Kirkland's striving for civilization. Particular household objects in the *Little House* books are depicted as conveying gentility, including a china shepherdess and a red-checked tablecloth. Both items traveled to the family's successive abodes in Kansas, Minnesota, and Dakota. As their daughters grew older, the Ingalls family also purchased an organ for their claim shanty. This striving for refinement, as has been noted, did not seem to have the same hold on Laura Smith.[15]

Perhaps most importantly, the direction of the *Little House* books is toward the development of responsibility during childhood, coming of age, and young adult life.[16] By contrast, the orientation of *Almost Pioneers* is toward early marriage and early motherhood. The final book in

---

14 See especially chapters 19 and 28 in *These Happy Golden Years*.

15 For the fascinating story of one Western woman who still strove for gentility in the most difficult of circumstances on the West's mining frontier—including reading Shakespeare—see Anne Ellis, *The Life of an Ordinary Woman* (Boston: Houghton Mifflin, 1990, first published 1929).

16 In fact, Pamela Smith Hill argues that Wilder helped to create the genre of young adult fiction (Hill, 173–175).

Wilder's series closes with Laura's contentment at her surroundings on her and Almanzo's farm the evening they were married:

> *Laura's heart was full of happiness. She knew she need never be homesick for the old home. It was so near that she could go to it whenever she wished, while she and Almanzo made the new home in their own little house.*
>
> *All this was theirs; their own horses, their own cow, their own claim. The many leaves of their little trees rustled softly in the gentle breeze. . . .*
>
> *"It is a wonderful night," Almanzo said.*
>
> *"It is a beautiful world," Laura answered. . . .*[17]

Wilder's books have a clear trajectory toward marriage and making her own home like the little houses created by her parents. The action in Smith's book mainly concerns making the best of their circumstances while living in Wyoming. By the end, there is a slight feeling of restlessness, of impatience to get to the next big thing. These points of difference between Laura Gibson Smith and Laura Ingalls Wilder reinforce the understanding of Laura Smith as a visitor to the West, not as a resident.

A final author that provides illustrative comparisons and contrasts to Laura Smith's narrative is Elinore Pruitt Stewart. Elinore Pruitt was born in White Bead Hill, Oklahoma, on June 3, 1876. Her parents had both died by the time she was fourteen, and she grew up with several of her siblings before marrying Harry Cramer Rupert in around 1902. Their daughter Jerrine was born in 1906. Later that year, Elinore was on her own with her daughter. While she later claimed that her husband had died in a railroad accident, historians have suggested that they actually divorced. By 1908 she was in Denver, working as

---

17   *These Happy Golden Years*, 289.

a housekeeper for Mrs. Coney, a "well-to-do and widowed school-teacher from Boston." She also worked intermittently as a laundress and a furnace tender. Nevertheless, survival was difficult for a single woman with a small child in the early twentieth century, and Elinore often found herself at the door of the City Rescue Mission. In 1909, she answered a *Denver Post* advertisement for a housekeeper placed by Clyde Stewart, a rancher from south-central Wyoming. In April of that year, Elinore moved to Burnt Fork, Wyoming, to live with Clyde. She filed on a homestead next to his land, and six weeks after her arrival, she married him and became Elinore Pruitt Stewart.[18]

Between 1909 and 1913, Stewart wrote twenty-six letters to her former employer, Mrs. Coney. They must have had a close relationship, because Mrs. Coney wrote back and sent gifts to both Elinore and her daughter Jerrine on birthdays and at Christmas. Elinore's letters are full of descriptions of the natural beauty of the Wyoming plains and mountains. She describes some of the day-to-day work on the ranch, but the letters are much more likely to provide details of camping trips that she took to visit neighbors, or for enjoyment. Her descriptions of nature are so vivid and her assessment of human foibles so lively, that Mrs. Coney had the letters published by *The Atlantic Monthly*. The letters were then released in book form by Houghton Mifflin in 1914, as *Letters from a Woman Homesteader*.[19] Thus, Stewart was writing about her life in Wyoming only a few years before the Smiths arrived in the state. Stewart's last letter is dated November 1913, when Laura and Earle were getting ready to return to Iowa after their first fall on their homestead. As a result, the works cry out for comparison.

---

18   Susanne K. George, *The Adventures of the Woman Homesteader: The Life and Letters of Elinore Pruitt Stewart* (Lincoln: University of Nebraska, 1992), 1–15; Sherry L. Smith, "Single Women Homesteaders: The Perplexing Case of Elinore Pruitt Stewart," *The Western Historical Quarterly* 22(2) (May 1991): 166–167.

19   Elinore Pruitt Stewart, *Letters of a Woman Homesteader* (Boston: Houghton Mifflin, 1988, first published 1914); George, 17–20, 28.

However, what one finds when comparing Stewart's work with Smith's are mostly contrasts. Part of this is due to the nature of the works and the identities of the women. Stewart wrote letters to a particular person, and as a result her narratives are shaped for that audience of one. Mrs. Coney was not a family member but a close friend, and Stewart's letters to her emphasized the unique, offbeat, and surprising nature of her experiences, especially her travels and interactions with interesting individuals. By contrast, Smith emphasizes the ordinariness of many of her experiences. Smith's account was also written some time after the events described, so the amount of detail is less than what's found in Stewart's lengthy and colorful descriptions of landscape, people, and objects.

The most striking difference between the two women and their accounts, however, comes from the commitment to Christianity that runs through Stewart's work. Stewart was a devout Roman Catholic, and there are many biblical allusions throughout her letters. She likens a sheepherder who wrote poetry to David the psalmist, and she describes the temptation to return to the comforts of Denver in the same terms as the Bible describes the temptation of the Old Testament Israelites to return to Egypt. She even read the book of Job aloud to an isolated farmer who asked her to read his family Bible.[20] Stewart describes preparing a neighborhood child for burial and conducting a funeral service herself, since there was no pastor nearby:

A dear little child has joined the angels. I dressed him and helped to make his casket. There is no minister in this whole country and I could not bear the little broken lilybud to be just carted away and buried, so I arranged the funeral and conducted the services. I know I am unworthy and in no way fitted for such a mission, but I did my poor best, and if no one else is comforted, I am. I know the message of

20 Stewart, 9, 11, 40, 92, 118.

God's love and care has been told once, anyway, to people who have learned to believe more strongly in hell than in heaven.[21]

This deep piety provides an obvious contrast to Earle Smith's halting recitation of the Twenty-Third Psalm and Lord's Prayer in chapter 13, and Laura's concern that the visiting preacher give earthly hope to those who had settled in their neighborhood in chapter 22. In a later letter, Stewart confides to Mrs. Coney that the child was actually her son. Stewart faithfully prays her rosary with her daughter, and she is happy to recite evening prayers with a Mexican family that they visit.[22]

There are some similarities, however, between Stewart's letters and Smith's memoir. Both had significant resources for settling in Wyoming. Earle and Laura had money from an inheritance mentioned in chapter 5. Stewart's choice to marry Clyde Stewart provided her with much more resources than most woman homesteaders would have had. In addition, both Laura and Elinore were happy to describe their different neighbors in bemused tones. There is greater ethnic diversity in Stewart's neighbors, which include a German woman, an Irish couple, some Scots, an English sheepherder, a French squatter, and a Mexican family. However, Smith's description of her neighbors, such as the Casters, Days, and Gillaspies, are similarly kind, human, and humorous.[23]

Ultimately, however, Stewart was a real rancher's wife and a settler. She had cast her lot in with those who lived in Wyoming, and she was committed to the work necessary to make her home a productive place. As such, Elinore describes undertaking men's work, and

---

21 Stewart, 98–99.

22 Stewart, 152, 190–191.

23 For a description of the many different ethnic groups present in southern Wyoming in 1920, see Brown, *Wyoming: A Geography*, 133–135, and Roy A. Jordan and S. Brett DeBoer, *Wyoming: A Source Book* (Niwot: University Press of Colorado, 1996), 60–61.

cultivating her successful garden.[24] Smith, on the other hand, was only "almost" a pioneer. She and Earle were not going to stay. They were visitors in Wyoming, not settlers. They grew the minimum of wheat necessary to gain title to the land, and she let her garden fail.

Together, Kirkland, Wilder, and Stewart left accounts of frontier Michigan in the early nineteenth century, frontier South Dakota near the close of the century, and frontier Wyoming during the first decades of the twentieth century. Like them, Laura Gibson Smith has given us a faithful depiction of her adventure in the West.

---

24   Stewart, 15–17, 279–282.

Index

Italicized page numbers indicate photographs. Footnotes are indicated with "n" followed by the footnote number.

About the Editor

John J. Fry is the chair of the history department at Trinity Christian College in Palos Heights, Illinois, in the southwestern suburbs of Chicago. He lives a block south of the city of Chicago in Blue Island, with his wife Paula and their four children. John has written a book about farmers in the American Midwest and what they were reading at the turn of the twentieth century, *The Farm Press, Reform, and Rural Change, 1895-1920*. His primary field of interest is the American West and rural history. Other interests include Western women writers, especially Laura Ingalls Wilder. He has also written on a variety of other topics, including Abraham Lincoln, Henry A. Wallace, and the 1950s. He regularly teaches courses on American history, Western civilization, American colonial and revolutionary history, twentieth-century America, and historical methods.